Song of Lawino & Song of Ocol

Ocol's tongue is fierce like the
arrow of the scorpion ...

SONG OF LAWINO
& SONG OF OCOL

OKOT p'BITEK

Introduction by G. A. Heron
Illustrations by Frank Horley

HEINEMANN

Heinemann Educational Publishers
Halley Court, Jordan Hill, Oxford OX2 8EJ
Part of Harcourt Education Limited

Heinemann is the registered trademark of
Harcourt Education Limited

Heinemann Publishers (Pty) Limited
PO Box 781940, Sandton 2146, Johannesburg, South Africa

British Library Cataloguing in Publication Data

p'Bitek, Okot
Song of Lawino & Song of Ocol.—African
writers series: 266)
1. English language—Translations from Acoli
2. Acoli poetry—Translations into English
I. Title   II. Series
896'.5   PL8041

ISBN 0-435-90266-0

Filmset in 10/11 pt Ehrhardt
Printed and bound in Great Britain by
Cox & Wyman Ltd, Reading, Berkshire

04 05 06 23 22 21

CONTENTS

INTRODUCTION

African writers who choose to use English or French set themselves certain problems. They wish to express African ideas, but they have chosen a non-African tool to express them. There is a grave danger that with the tool of language they will borrow other foreign things. Every language has its own stock of common images expressing a certain people's way of looking at things. Every language has its own set of literary forms which limit a writer's manner of expression. How many of these tools can a writer borrow before his African ideas are affected by the influence of foreign ideas implied in them?

The first few African writers in colonial countries were not concerned with this problem. They simply imitated and praised their conquerors.[1] But this group was small, short-lived and insignificant. Ever since the idea of 'negritude' emerged in the 1940s among French-speaking writers[2] most African writers have been conscious of the dangers. They have tried in various ways to mould European languages and forms so that they could express African ideas. The 'negritude' writers based their poems on images taken from African traditions. Chinua Achebe, one of the earliest successful English speaking writers, uses the European novel form, but he is very careful to create an 'Africanised' English for the dialogue of his characters.[3]

Despite these efforts, many European influences are present in African writing and in the criticism of African writing. Sadly, the written literature of the African nations has been clearly separated in many people's minds from the oral literary heritage that is present in every African community. Comparisons have more often been made between African poems and European poems than between African poems and traditional songs. Fortunately this emphasis is now changing.

Okot p'Bitek compels us to make comparisons between his poems and traditional songs. The title 'Song of . . .' that he has given to all his poems suggests the comparison. He used many features borrowed from traditional songs in the writing of *Song of Lawino*. Partly because of the familiarity of these features to all Africans, *Song of Lawino* has become one of the most successful African literary works. Some African writers have been read mainly by a small well-educated elite. Okot succeeded in reaching many people who rarely show an interest in written literature, while still winning praise from the elite for his poems.

This success seems remarkable if we consider the fact that some publishers rejected this poem only a few years before this achievement. These rejections probably came mainly from the publishers' familiarity with European rather than African forms of literature. But the idea of a long poem is now a rather strange one in either tradition. Few poets use long poems now. Again *Song of Lawino* does not fit into any Western model for a long poem. It is not an epic poem, it is not a narrative poem, it is not the private meditations of the poet. This written 'Song' form was born in Uganda while Okot was writing *Song of Lawino*.

If there was now only one 'Song', we could perhaps discount this originality of form as an insignificant accident. Okot, however, continued to write even longer poems. *Song of Ocol*, *Song of Prisoner* and *Song of Malaya* are all in similar form to *Song of Lawino*. In addition, two other writers were sufficiently impressed by *Song of Lawino* to write their own 'Songs'. Joseph Buruga in *The Abandoned Hut* is strongly influenced by Okot, and Okello Oculi in *Orphan* and *Malak* is experimenting in different ways to use long poems in English in an African way to express African emotions and problems. It is interesting to look further at these 'Songs' to see why they have made an impact.

An equally important reason for the success of these poems is the controversial issues that they raise. In some circles in East Africa, the words Lawino and Ocol have become common nouns. You will hear the 'Ocols' or the 'Lawinos' of Africa praised or condemned in many arguments. The two characters have become prototypes of two opposing approaches to the cultural future of Africa. You will have your own opinions in this debate and after you have enjoyed these poems you will be able to make up your own mind about the relevance of Okot's contribution to it. This introduction contains a short biography of the writer and a consideration of the influence of Acoli songs on *Song of Lawino*. Then I discuss some details of the form and imagery of the two poems. Finally I try to suggest some issues raised by the poems which may be discussed.

Biography

Okot p'Bitek was born in Gulu, northern Uganda, in 1931. He went to Gulu High School and King's College, Budo. In 1952, he went for a two year course at the Government Teacher Training College, Mbarara. He then taught English and Religious Knowledge at Sir Samuel Baker's School near Gulu. His parents were well-known people in the local Protestant community and in this period Okot also was a Christian. He was already interested in music, he was the choir-master at Sir Samuel Baker's School. He was also active in politics during this period.

His first venture into literature was a poem called 'The Lost Spear'. This poem retold the traditional Lwo tale of the spear, the bead and the bean. Okot wrote this while at Budo and Mbarara. He says the poem was very much influenced by Longfellow's *Hiawatha*, which Okot admired greatly. He lost this manuscript. However, in 1953, while still at Mbarara, he published a novel, *Lak Tar*, in the Acoli language.

Lak Tar tells the story of an Acoli boy whose father dies while he is still very young. A few years later he falls in love with a girl and she agrees to marry him, but he is unable to pay the very high bride-price. His stepfather and his uncles refuse to help him. The rest of the novel relates the series of misfortunes that befall him when he goes to Kampala to try to earn the money he needs. Despite nearly two years away, he earns only a fraction of the bride-price, and during his return journey he is robbed. The novel ends with his arrival home, miserable and penniless.

Okot's other major interest at this time was football. He played for his school, his college, local clubs, his district team and the Uganda national team. It was through this interest in football that he first travelled widely in northern Uganda. He made many friends and gained more varied experience of the traditions of his people which was later very useful to him. Football also helped him to travel even further afield. In 1958 he went with the Uganda team on a tour of Britain.

Okot took this opportunity to extend his education. He stayed in England to study. He did a one year course for a diploma in Education at Bristol University. He then did a degree course in Law at Aberystwyth. It was during this period that Okot lost his Christian commitment. It was also at this time that the direction of his interests changed from the European traditions he had been studying to the traditions of his own people. While studying the Medieval European tradition of trial by ordeal he recognised a parallel to the traditions of the Acoli. He wanted to investigate this.

When he finished his Law degree in 1962 he had an opportunity to pursue his interest in African traditions. He moved to Oxford University to study for a B.Litt. in social anthropology. It was in this period that he developed many of the attitudes he expresses strongly in his poems and academic works. In his Preface to his book *African Religions in Western Scholarship*, he tells us of his conflicts with his teachers:

> During the very first lecture ... the teacher kept referring to
> Africans or non-Western peoples as barbarians, savages,
> primitive tribes, etc. I protested, but to no avail.[5]

In this book he is strongly critical of the whole idea of social anthropology. He claims that anthropology has always been concerned to support and justify colonialism, and that it should therefore not be studied in African Universities.[6] This kind of rejection of Western traditions parallels his attempts to use African forms for his poetry.

The movement towards Ugandan independence persuaded Okot to return home for a short time in 1962. He intended to stand as the U.P.C. candidate for Gulu, but he changed his mind. While back in Uganda he took the opportunity to do some fieldwork for his B.Litt. degree. He then returned to Oxford. His research now centred mainly on the oral literature of his people. He completed his thesis *Oral Literature and its Background among the Acoli and Lang'o* in 1964. He then returned to work in Uganda.

First he worked in Gulu again, for the extra-mural department of Makerere College. He continued his research in traditional songs, especially investigating the religious ideas expressed through them. He was also involved with a large group of friends in the creation of the Gulu Festival. He was a performer as well as an organiser, singing and dancing with a group and devising ways of adapting traditional songs to the different performance conditions of the Festival. It was in this period that he wrote *Wer pa Lawino*, the Acoli version of *Song of Lawino*. It is easy to see how songs that Okot was working on could influence the composition of his own poem.

In 1966 he moved to Kampala. There he tried to carry on similar work by changing the emphasis of the Ugandan Cultural Centre from mainly foreign works to mainly traditional performances. He was involved from the beginning in the formation of a large and successful traditional dance group called 'The Heartbeat of Africa'. He was later appointed Director of the Uganda Cultural Centre. He organised an eight day Festival to coincide with the Independence celebrations in October 1968.

Shortly after this, his career in Uganda was abruptly cut short. While returning from a trip to Zambia he learnt that he had been dismissed. He was later told that his strong criticisms of politicians in *Song of Lawino* and elsewhere caused this dismissal. He left Uganda and went to work at the University of Nairobi, first in Kisumu and then in Nairobi. Okot packed a great deal of activity into his life, always working hard. In 1975 he published a collection of essays *Africa's Cultural Revolution*. A collection of Acoli songs was published as *The Horn of My Love* in 1974 and in 1978 a refreshing version of familiar tales, *Hare and Hornbill*. These widely different books are all united by Okot's concern that the nations of Africa should be built on African not European foundations. He returned to Makerere University as Professor of Creative Writing but tragically died in 1982 within five months of taking up the appointment.

Influence of Songs and Effect of Translation

Okot wrote the Acoli version of *Song of Lawino* in a period in his life when he was daily concerned with Acoli traditional songs, both in his research and in his activities in connection with the Gulu Festival. In his work for the Festival, he co-operated very closely with a large group of friends. These are some of the people whose help he acknowledged on the title pages of *Song of Lawino*. Naturally when Okot was writing his poem he also worked together with these friends. He read new versions of each chapter of the poem to these people as soon as they were completed, and their comments were taken into account if the chapter needed rewriting. Thus even its method of composition is similar to that of traditional songs. A group of singers work together and continuously alter the songs as they perform them.

Other elements link the poem to traditional songs. In most parts of

the poem, Lawino addresses herself to someone, for example:
'Husband' (p. 34), 'my clansmen' (p. 35), 'Brother' (p. 37). This
form of address is a rhetorical device taken straight from Acoli oral
literature. Another feature used a lot in *Wer pa Lawino* and sometimes
also occurring in the translation is the use of a repeated phrase as a
refrain, emphasising an important idea. There is a good example of
this in Chapter 3:

> Timme ducu lutimme Munu-Munu
> Ping'o lewic pe mako Munu,
> Lukwako dako atyer, calo Munu
> Luting'o pong' kor, calo Munu
> Wumato taa cigara, calo Munu,
> Wa mon, wa co calo Munu;
> Wunato lem-wu calo Munu,
> Wunato dog-wu calo Munu,
> Wunango laa dogwu calo Munu,
> Ma dog co nywak ki reng'ng'e pa Munu.[7]

In the English version this repetition is considerably reduced:

> You kiss her on the cheek
> As white people do,
> You kiss her open-sore lips
> As white people do
> You suck the slimy saliva
> From each other's mouths
> As white people do. (p. 44)

This translates only three lines of the original. In the translation of
the other lines the refrain is missed out. This repetition can be used
over a few lines, as in this example, or to tie together a whole chapter.
The repetition of this phrase strongly emphasises the idea of slavish
imitation which Lawino finds so ridiculous in the dance.

The whole of the poem is tied together by a similar refrain. It is
taken from an Acoli proverb. In *Wer pa Lawino* it reads:

> Te Okono obur bong' luputu.[8]

Okot's translation is:

> The pumpkin in the old homestead
> Must not be uprooted! (p. 41)

Pumpkins are a luxury food. They grow wild throughout Acoliland. To uproot pumpkins, even when you are moving to a new homestead, is simple wanton destruction. In this proverb, then, Lawino is not asking Ocol to cling to everything in his past, but rather not to destroy things for the sake of destroying them. Again, the refrain is used to emphasise an important idea the writer is putting across in the whole poem.

The most important influence Acoli songs have had on *Song of Lawino* is in the imagery Okot uses. Okot has completely avoided the stock of common images of English literature through his familiarity with the stock of common images of Acoli literature. In the English version, this gives his poem a feeling of freshness for every reader, and a sense of Africanness for African readers. One place where these images are found in the poem are in the quotations for songs that are set out as quotations in the text. There are examples of these on pages 60; 62; 66–7; 76–8; 98; 101; 115; 120. These songs often convey Lawino's feelings more fully than her own words. The song on page 83, for example, expresses the sorrow in the names of sadness very clearly:

> Fate has brought troubles
> Son of my mother
> Fate has thrown me a basket,
> It all began as a joke
> Suffering is painful
> It began before I was born.

More important than these are the innumerable places where Lawino's own words echo the words of a traditional song. If we look at a few lines of *Song of Lawino* next to a few lines from an Acoli song, we can see this clearly:

Beg forgiveness from them	The spear with the hard point
And ask them to give you	Slits the granite rock
A new spear	The spear that I trust
A new spear with a sharp and hard point	Penetrates the granite rock
A spear that will crack the rock	The hunter has slept in the wilderness
Ask for a spear that you will trust (p. 119)	I die oh,[9]

Through his thorough knowledge of an African literary tradition Okot has succeeded in using English as a tool to reach a wider audience without borrowing foreign elements that distort his message.

All but a very few lines of *Song of Lawino* were written in Acoli originally and later translated into English. For most parts of the poem, the translation was an afterthought. When Okot was trying to publish the Acoli version, he translated a small extract for a writer's conference in Nairobi. The enthusiastic reception of this persuaded him to translate the whole poem. *Song of Ocol* was also an afterthought. Lawino was an unsuitable spokesman for one or two of Okot's comments on the East African scene. *Song of Ocol* was needed to add this extra dimension. *Song of Ocol* was written in English throughout; there is no Acoli version.

Okot's 'Songs' are not songs in any literal sense. You cannot sing them. They are not simply a written version of Acoli songs. Acoli songs do not grow to book length. They are one or two verses repeated with musical accompaniment. They are not written down under one person's authorship. They are sung and adapted by singer after singer, and each singer is free to create in his own way and change the song to fit current events or refer to his own girl-friend. They do not use rhyme or the regular rhythm used in *Wer pa Lawino*.

So it is possible to exaggerate the influence of Acoli tradition on Okot's poems. From western tradition he takes the idea of individual authorship, of spoken verse, of rhyme, of division into chapters, of the printed word. But many of the aspects that give them their impact are those aspects which are a direct continuation of his people's own tradition. Okot has adapted a traditional form to new conditions of performance, rather than created a new form.

The writer chose to make a very literal translation of *Song of Lawino*. The main differences between the two versions are the rearrangement of the order of certain sections within the chapters, the filling out of some descriptions of things unfamiliar to readers of the English version, and the dropping from the English version of some details which are in the Acoli original. There is no doubt that, as Taban lo Liyong has said:

the meaning of deep Acoli proverbs are made very light by their rendition into English word for word, rather than sense for sense, or proverb for proverb.[10]

Certain areas of meaning are lost through this kind of translation. If we take the lines:

> The pumpkin in the old homestead
> Must not be uprooted ... (p. 41)

it is obvious that, even after an explanation, non-Acoli readers will not feel the force of the proverb as Acoli readers would. And the poem is full of such references to songs, carrying meanings that have been built up over years of familiarity with the words. It is possible that with a longer, less literal, translation some of this meaning could have been retained, but the result would have been very cumbersome.

But the advantages of Okot's method outweigh these disadvantages. As I have pointed out, many African writers using English or French have attempted to 'Africanise' these languages. Okot p'Bitek has succeeded in this more than any other previous writer. A less literal translation would have involved the intrusion of foreign elements into his poem. It is true that Okot's 'Acoli-English'[11] carries deeper meaning to Acoli readers than to others, but it is rarely obscure for Africans.

There are occasions when Okot deliberately adds strangeness in the translation which is not there in the original. The most obvious example of this is in Chapter 8. Instead of using the biblical terms, 'gospel', 'Holy Ghost', 'God', Okot gives us a literal retranslation of the Acoli translation of these words. So we have: 'good word' (p. 73), 'clean ghost' (p. 74) and strangest of all 'the Hunchback' (p. 75). Here the English version carries the strangeness of these words to Lawino when she first heard them more strongly than the Acoli version. Most Acoli readers will be familiar with the Christian meaning of these terms and will not find them strange at all.

If we look at the first few pages of Chapter 4 (p. 47), we can see a more normal example of Okot's translation working well. The first 74 lines of this chapter (up to: "Should they open it/So that the pus may flow out?") correspond more or less exactly in ideas to the first 49 lines of the Acoli version. One or two details in the description of the house and the abuse of Ocol that are in the original are missing in the translation. The arrangement of the passage has also been slightly changed. The Acoli version uses *'diro me Acoli'* or *'ryeko me Acoli'* (the skill or wisdom of the Acoli)[12] as a refrain in a very tight description of the home. This repetition is missing from the English version, and the description is filled out with a little explanation, as the scene is unfamiliar to non-Acoli readers.

Okot leaves two words untranslated: '*Lyonno* and *nyadyang*'. These give the passage a feeling of strangeness without making it difficult to understand. The passage contains a quotation from a song:

> Father prepare the kraal etc. (p. 48)

and also an image borrowed from another song:

> And my name blew
> Like a horn
> Among the Payira. (p. 48)

Okot does not explain the reference to the expected bride-price of cattle but this will present no difficulty to Africans. In this section, Okot gets the advantages of a literal translation with very little loss of meaning.

Verse

In *Song of Lawino* Okot replaces the regular rhythm and rhyme of the Acoli version with irregular free verse in the English version. His lines in *Song of Lawino* usually end with a strong emphasis. He builds his lines around the words he wants to emphasise, crowding weaker words into the beginning of the line:

> They mould the tips of the cotton nests
> So that they are sharp
> And with these they prick
> The chests of their men (p. 39)

This gives a staccato effect to his verse. This can be clumsy, but it sometimes successfully underlines Lawino's contemptuous moods:

> He just shouts
> Like house-flies
> Settling on top of excrement
> When disturbed. (p. 49)

The arrangement of the verse suits Lawino's feelings.

Sometimes Okot successfully softens these lines to convey Lawino's wistful moods. The section from the beginning of Chapter 4 illustrates this. While she remembers Ocol's wooing of her and the beauty of her home, Lawino's voice takes on a note of nostalgia (p. 47). The staccato effect of the lines is reduced in sympathy. There are soft sounds ending many of the lines, for example: 'briskly', 'lily', 'cattle', 'silently'. The lines flow smoothly to express Lawino's gentler mood.

In *Song of Ocol* the emphatic stresses at the end of Okot's lines are replaced by much more varied patterns of stress. The lines are shorter and Okot often misses out structural words which sometimes crowd out the lines in *Song of Lawino*. Okot also makes very effective use of one or two syllable lines to provide shock changes of pace. This changes the staccato effect into a lively bouncing rhythm:

> You sister
> From Pokot
> Who grew in the open air
> You are fresh ...
> Ah!
> Come,
> Walk with me ... (p. 138).

Song of Ocol is very easy to read aloud. In this poem Okot shows himself to be a master of English free verse.

The language and imagery of *Song of Ocol* lack the references to oral tradition which give *Song of Lawino* some of its richness, but Okot shows himself well able to create his own imagery. One source of pleasure in the poem is the poet's evident delight in the use of words. The images crowd on top of one another so that the reader's imagination is feasted on a succession of vivid pictures:

> Mad creature
> Her hair
> A burnt out forest
> Her eyes
> Shooting out from the head
> A pair of rockets
> Serpent tongues
> Spitting poison
> Lashing crocodile tail ... (p. 127).

The Character of Lawino

The character of Lawino dominates *Song of Lawino* and it is important for you to consider how successful Okot's portrait of her is. The poem is based on a real social problem, very common in rural areas in East Africa. Many wives have seen their husbands move out of the range of their education and experience through travel. Many 'Ocols' return home with nothing but contempt for the ways of their parents and their wives. What we need to consider is whether Lawino's response to this situation is 'real'. Does she react in the way we would expect women in such a situation to react?

To consider her character, we can divide the poem fairly easily into three sections. In the first five chapters Lawino is a perfect portrait of a woman scorned. She lashes out at Ocol, who used to admire her, and Clementine, who has usurped her place, indiscriminately. Then Tina disappears. In Chapters 6 to 11, Lawino seems much less concerned with her personal plight. She defends the customs of her ancestors with more and more profound comparisons between Western and Acoli ways. The last two chapters tie the concerns of the other two sections together. Lawino's desire to win back Ocol's admiration is combined with a commentary on the whole Acoli community and an appeal for the renewal of traditional ways.

I find the Lawino of the first five chapters extremely credible. She is not jealous of Clementine in the narrow sense of desiring to have sole possession of Ocol. She is familiar with polygamy, she knows no other form of marriage. She is simply mystified and annoyed that Ocol prefers a woman who is no younger than her and can match her in none of her womanly accomplishments. Her mystification finds expression in wistful descriptions of her own beauty, and her annoyance in abuse of everything she has seen or heard of Ocol's new way of life.

I think the sudden disappearance of Tina weakens the portrait of Lawino a little. I think it is this slight change in emphasis which has led some critics to make a distinction between Lawino as the woman scorned and Lawino as the defender of Acoli customs. In his review of *Wer pa Lawino* Okumu pa Lukobo says:

In choosing as his text *Ter okon bong' luputu* (Don't uproot the pumpkin) I think Bitek has made a mistake. What Lawino has to say would have been better expressed by another Acoli proverb which says *Dako abila ni eye meni* (Your first wife is your mother). For what Lawino is really concerned with is a personal matter—her rivalry with her husband's mistress Kelementina.[13]

This seems to me to be a misunderstanding of a very common feature of literature. Both oral and written literatures often operate at the same time on different levels of meaning. A domestic situation may be used by a singer or a writer to make a political comment. I see no contradiction between Lawino as an offended first wife and Lawino as the defender of Acoli values.

In fact, I think that a great deal of the appeal of *Song of Lawino* comes from Okot's exploitation of the dramatic possibilities of Lawino's rivalry with Clementine. Other writers have satirised aspects of life together or appealed to such a wide audience. Part of this success is due to the credibility of his portrait of Lawino.

Nevertheless, by allowing Tina to disappear completely from the poem, Okot gives some slight justification to these critics. But it should be pointed out that Lawino is concerned mainly to attack Ocol, and that Ocol is very clearly present in every part of the poem. Unlike Ocol in *Son of Ocol*, she doesn't shift from attacks on one group of people to attacks on another. Throughout the poem she is mocking Ocol. The domestic situation and the character of Lawino in themselves provide a fairly consistent level of meaning in the poem. This level of meaning contributes to the success of Okot's more serious aims in the poem.

Lawino as Spokesman

If *Song of Lawino* were no more than a good picture of a woman from an Acoli village it would not have attracted all the attention that has been devoted to it in the few years since its publication. Lawino is the writer's tool for making his own comments on the way people behave in East Africa. At first sight it may seem that he has chosen a very bad tool. Certainly Taban lo Liyong, when he wrote *The Last Word*, thought so. He wrote:

Africans have been mad at expatriates for taking the African houseboy as the representative African. Okot hasn't done better by letting a mere catechist criticise the West and Westernisation. . . . The trouble with his method is that his discussion is conducted in a low key; it is the simple that he deals with ... things to be seen with the eyes, things to be heard with the ears, or felt with the skin—but little to be felt with the intellect.[14]

There is some truth in this. One of the reaons why Ocol's reply was necessary is that Okot couldn't say all he wanted to through Lawino because of her limited experience.

However, Lawino manages remarkably well. Because she is not intellectual, it does not mean she is not intelligent. Though she always uses simple language, as we shall see, she raises most of the issues about Westernisation that an intellectual might have raised. More important, Lawino's ignorance enables Okot to do something which more intellectual poems failed to do.

In his book *African Religions in Western Scholarship*, Okot talks of the 'systematic and intensive use of dirty gossip'[15] by Western scholars in describing the ways of life of Africans. Whether or not Okot is scrupulously fair to all Western scholars, it is clear that much of the disruption and cruelty of colonial rule was made possible by white men's ignorance of African ways of living and their preparedness to accept the tales they invented round their dinner tables as the truth. The sad thing is that some Africans still exaggerate ridiculous aspects of traditional ways without acknowledging valuable aspects of them.

To a considerable extent, Lawino uses 'dirty gossip' against her enemies. Because she is not 'intellectual' she lacks the ability imaginatively to project herself into Western culture which African intellectuals, through their enforced exposure to Western education, usually possess. In relation to Western culture she is a complete outsider. Even a character like the house servant in Oyono's *Houseboy*, though he eventually violently rejects it, has much more sympathy with Western culture than Lawino. Because of this, Lawino is free to turn the Western weapon of 'dirty gossip' back on its users. It is natural for her to express the prejudices of her people. And these prejudices are simply the negative expression of her positive beliefs. By using Lawino, Okot is able to present Acoli ideas without the awareness of the other side's case which hampers some of the more intellectual approaches.

Lawino is not unfair to Europeans. She is not trying to impose her set of beliefs on them. She is using her prejudices in an argument with other Africans within Africa. But she is unreasonable in some of her criticism of Clementine and Ocol. Some of her comments are little more than scandal-mongering. For example, in Chapter 2, when she first attacks Clementine, the climax of her abuse is:

> Perhaps she has aborted many!
> Perhaps she has thrown her twins
> In the pit latrine! (p. 39)

The word 'perhaps' shows that Lawino is simply spreading a tale against Clementine. Again some of her accusations against Ocol are a little unlikely. She says:

> Perhaps you are covering up
> Your bony hips and chest
> And the large scar on your thigh
> And the scabies on your buttocks. (p. 50)

The word 'perhaps' is there again.

Even through this kind of abuse Lawino is expressing aspects of African tradition. Abortion is now legal in some Western countries. The concern with population control in those countries outweighs the dislike most people feel for the operation. With the African attitude to the event of birth and and the respect of all traditions for large familes, the whole idea of abortion in any circumstances is abhorrent. Again, in a society where very few clothes are normally worn, the only people who cover themselves are those who are ashamed of their bodies.

This abuse is another factor which links *Song of Lawino* to traditional literature. One function that traditional songs and stories sometimes fulfil is to enable members of a family or community to step outside the normal restraints which their family roles impose on what they say to one another. In a song, the singer is free to use mockery to criticise the conduct of other members of the community, and especially to deflate the self-important. Such a singer is always likely to overstate his case. This is exactly what Lawino does in her abuse of Ocol in this poem.

Through this kind of overstatement, Okot took African poetry from defence to attack. Colonialists have been attacked for their oppressive policies in innumerable novels and poems. Certain glaring failings of Western culture were exposed by some works. But much of the writing before *Song of Lawino* was primarily defensive in its cultural comparisons. Many writers were involved mainly in telling the white man 'we too have a culture.' The first necessary exercise was to defend African culture from the abuses heaped on it by the colonialists.

This kind of writing has produced some excellent work, but it can have limitations. Many of you will have read Camara Laye's *The African Child*. This book has its good points, but its picture of African life is incomplete. For example, the writer plays down throughout the book the fact that his father was polygamous. He didn't want to spoil the favourable impression of African ways he was trying to give to French readers by references to something that might offend them. There is no such equivocation in *Song of Lawino*. Acoli ways are presented without apology, systematically compared to European ways and consistently found to be better. Lawino is proud, not only of her beauty, but of every aspect of her way of life. From this position of pride she attacks.

We can see this very well if we consider Lawino's attitude to sexual morality. The 'dirty gossip' of the colonialists condemned African dances because of the immorality of nakedness. Lawino doesn't waste her time on a reasoned and balanced defence of dancing naked. She presents the openness, liveliness and healthiness of the Acoli dance positively, without apology:

> When the drums are throbbing
> And the black youths
> Have raised much dust
> You dance with vigour and health
> You dance naughtily with pride
> You dance with spirit,
> You compete, you insult, you provoke
> You challenge all! (p. 42)

Then she goes to the attack:

> Each man has a woman
> Although she is not his wife,
> They dance inside a house
> And there is no light.
> Shamelessly, they hold each other
> Tightly, tightly,
> They cannot breathe. (p. 44)

Western dances are immoral because people embrace in public and dance with anyone, even close relatives.

The same question of sexual morality is involved in her later comments on Catholic priests and nuns. The tradition of priestly celibacy has a long history in Europe. There is also a long tradition of priestly hypocrisy, and of literary mockery of this hypocrisy. But still the idea of celibacy has a serious basis in many people's minds and has been and still is, to a lesser extent, a familiar and influential idea in European culture. To Lawino the whole idea is completely incomprehensible. As Okot pointed out in *African Religions in Western Scholarship:*[16]

> ... the African viewpoint ... takes sex as a good thing.

So when the Padre and the Nun shout at her, it must be their sexual frustration expressing itself·

> They are angry with me
> As if it was I
> Who prevented them marrying ... (p. 85)

Again no priest can possibly discipline his sexual desires. The teacher from the Evening Speaker's Class follows her to the dance. (p. 81). And every teacher must be like this:

> And all the teachers
> Are alike
> They have sharp eyes
> For girls' full breasts ...

Lawino turns on her attackers and exposes their own immorality and hypocrisy.

These attacks on western ways are another reason for the popular success of the poem. They make the poem lively and readable and give the shock effect of a first reading. The ridicule is firmly based on African ways of looking at things; many students will have heard this kind of thing in their village. The shock comes from seeing it on the printed page. Many students will be more familiar with condemnation of nakedness in dances than with mockery of Westernised dances.

Okot is making a number of very serious points through Lawino's mockery of Westernised ways. At its mildest he is saying that the idea of 'progress' cannot be applied to culture. Ocol thinks that Acoli ways of dress, dance and religion are 'primitive' and must be superseded. But Lawino shows ways in which western things can be dirty, stupid or hypocritical. At the same time she shows how traditional ways of life allow her to express herself fully and freely as a woman. Both ways of life are open to criticism, both ways of life are valid. If Lawino has learnt one way of life, why should she change? Why should the Masai wear trousers? The words like 'witch', 'Kaffirs' and 'scorcerers' that Ocol throws at her don't answer that question.

But Lawino doesn't believe that the two ways of life are equally valid for Africans, and neither does Okot. She thinks the customs of white people probably suit white people. She doesn't mind them following their own ways.

> I do not understand
> The ways of foreigners
> But I do not despise their customs. (p. 41)

She doesn't expect them to want to imitate her:

> ... no white woman
> Wishes to do her hair
> Like mine,
> Because she is proud
> Of the hair with which she was born ... (p. 56)

But those Africans who insist on following the ways of white people are foolish, because they misunderstand their own ways and do not know themselves. If they try to destroy African traditions, they will fail:

> Listen Ocol, my old friend,
> The ways of your ancestors
> Are good,
> Their customs are solid
> And not hollow
> They are not thin, not easily breakable
> They cannot be blown away
> By the winds
> Because their roots reach deep into the soil. (p. 41)

In the later chapters of *Song of Lawino* and in *Song of Ocol*, Okot shows us clearly what he thinks happens to those people who try to destroy their own roots. We can understand his points best if we look at the character of Ocol.

The Character of Ocol

If we read *Song of Lawino* carefully a clear picture of the character of Ocol emerges. In *Song of Ocol*, Ocol, out of his own mouth, confirms Lawino's view of him. In many places throughout *Song of Lawino* Lawino asserts that Ocol is rude and abusive both to her and to other people:

> My husband abuses me together with my parents
> He says terrible things about my mother ... (p. 35)

In *Song of Ocol*, Ocol confirms this impression. Rather than reasoning with Lawino he just shouts insults and throws her out of his house:

> Song of the woman
> Is sour sweet
> It is pork gone rancid,
> It is the honeyed
> Bloodied sour milk
> In the stinking
> Maasai gourd. (p. 124)

In Chapter 7, when a beggar predicts violent revolution, Ocol, the politician, makes no attempt to reason with him, but simply insults the man:

> Out of my way
> You cowardly fool
> Creep back and hide
> In your mother's womb ... (p. 145)

Ocol is 'arrogant' (p. 35).

But Ocol's arrogance and self-importance do not give him dignity. He is always in a hurry. He is ruled by time. Everything he does must take place at a fixed time:

> ... my husband insists
> What exact time
> He should have morning tea
> When exactly to have coffee ... (p. 64).

Lawino doesn't understand the need for these set times. She does things when she wants to. Children are fed or washed when it is necessary (p. 69), and:

> When sleep comes
> Into their heads
> They sleep ... (p. 69)

Why make your life harder by fixing times for everything? It just confuses her.

For the Acoli times is not a commodity that can be consumed until it is finished:

> In the wisdom of the Acoli
> Time is not stupidly split up
> Into seconds and minutes
> It does not flow
> Like beer in a pot
> That is sucked
> Until it is finished. (p. 69)

If visitors come when you are doing something you stop and enjoy their visit. But Ocol has no time to enjoy anything:

> He never jokes
> With anybody
> He says
> He has no time
> To sit around the evening fire. (p. 67)

All his life is haunted by his fear of wasting time. For Ocol, time is a commodity which can be bought and sold. It must not be wasted because:

> Time is money. (p. 67)

When visitors appear at his door Ocol tries to get rid of them quickly with the question:

> What can I do for you? (p. 68)

and even the crying of children makes him wild with rage because it interrupts his work (p. 67). Despite his high opinion of himself he is no more than a servant of time:

Time has become
My husband's master ... (p. 68)

and no one is likely to respect him because he:

... runs from place to place
Like a small boy. (p. 68)

Other people don't share Ocol's views of his own importance.

Time is not Ocol's only master. He is a politician, and before the
leaders of his party he behaves like:

... a newly-eloped girl ... (p. 108)

Ocol says in his speeches that he is fighting for national unity:

He says
They want to unite the Acoli and Lang'o
And the Madi and the Lugbara
Should live together in peace! (p. 103)

But his political energies don't really seem to be geared towards bringing
about unity, national or local. Most of his time as a politician is taken
up with condemning other people. Ocol says that the Congress Party
is against all Catholics, and that they will steal all their property, if
elected:

(They) ... will take people's wives
And goats and chickens and bicycles,
All will become the property
Of the Congress people. (pp. 105–6)

And it is not only the other party that he condemns. When he talks
to the party leaders, he:

... accuses other party leaders
Everybody else is useless,
He alone
Is the most hard working ... (p. 108)

The most destructive result of his political activity is its effect on
his own family. Ocol's brother is in the Congress party. Because of
this their former closeness is replaced by enmity. Ocol thinks his brother
wants to murder him (p. 105). He forbids Lawino to talk to the

Introduction

man who may one day become her husband (p. 105). Politics has destroyed the unity of home and brought misery to every member of it:

> The women there
> Wear mourning clothes
> The homestead is surely dead ... (p. 111)

Ocol's political activity has only created new conflicts without settling the old ones.

And the material benefits that might partially compensate for these new conflicts are only enjoyed by the few, only by the strong:

> ... if your chest
> Is small, bony and weak
> They push you off ... (p. 107)

This is the most important division brought by the political activities which followed Uhuru, the division between the rich, who have the politicians' favour, and the poor, who have nothing:

> And those who have
> Fallen into things
> Throw themselves into soft beds,
> But the hip bones of the voters
> Grow painful
> Sleeping on the same earth
> They slept
> Before Uhuru. (p. 110)

The politicians, Okot says, are doing nothing about this division. They are too busy fighting one another.

Certainly Ocol sees no reason to do anything. In Chapter 6 of *Song of Ocol* he asks the voters to agree that because he has worked harder for Uhuru he deserves:

> Some token reward. (p. 139)

The reward he has taken for himself is a large house in the town and a big farm in the country (p. 139 and 141). He is not responsible for the sufferings of the voters:

> Is it my fault
> That you sleep
> In a hut
> With a leaking thatch? (p. 139)

Why should Uhuru bring them wealth? They are just expecting too much. There must be powerful people and weak people and they can't be expected to mix:

> Have lions
> Begun to eat grass
> To lie down with lambs
> And to play games with antelopes? (p. 142)

To Ocol these new divisions in African societies seem natural.

In Chapter 10 we are given further examples of Ocol's intolerance. Ocol will let neither Lawino's relatives, nor his own relatives into his house because they might make it dirty (p. 91) or give diseases to his children (p. 91). He condemns all traditional medicines. If they are occasionally effective it must be:

> ... by accident ... (p. 93)

Again, he condemns all traditional religious beliefs, because he is an educated man and a Christian. In the years since independence there has been a great deal of reassessment of the missionaries' views of African traditional beliefs by African Christians. Many Christians now see much that is of value in these beliefs.[17] Ocol's attitudes have not changed at all. For him traditional beliefs are no more than 'foolish superstitions' (p. 92).

Ocol not only rejects these 'superstitions' himself; he wants to wipe them out. He prevents Lawino from visiting the diviner priest or making sacrifices when she is in trouble (p. 93). When his father was alive, he:

> Once smashed up the rattle gourd
> Cut open the drum
> And chased away the diviner priest
> From his late father's homestead. (p. 95)

He later tried to destroy the tree on his father's shrine (p. 95). Yet Ocol is a religious man. Lawino must not wear charms, yet he wears a crucifix (p. 93). Prayer can be effective:

> It is stupid superstition
> To pray to our ancestors
> To avert the smallpox
> But we should pray
> To the messengers of the Hunchback
> To intercede for us. (p. 93)

Ocol sees no similarity between the two sorts of charms or the two sorts of prayer.

In Chapter 9 we see another aspect of Ocol's arrogance. Lawino here asks questions in a genuine mood of enquiry. And she does not ask 'silly questions' (p. 87). The problem of who created the Creator and the mystery of the virgin birth are problems which better educated people have found to be barriers to Christian belief. An educated Christian like Ocol ought to have considered them. His casual refusal to discuss them because Lawino is not educated is a lame excuse. If he were really interested in knowledge he would be willing to discuss these things. But Lawino doesn't think he is really interested in knowledge. She wishes she had someone else to ask:

> Someone who has genuinely
> Read deeply and widely
> And not someone like my husband
> Whose preoccupation
> Is to boast in the market place ... (p. 90)

What has this man gained from his education?

Lawino really makes us wonder whether this 'progressive and civilised man' (p. 36) deserves any respect. With all his status he surely ought to have a little more diginity. He surely ought to be more patient and tolerant. Above all he ought to treat his wife, his parents and his home community with a little more respect. In Chapters 8 and 12 we have Lawino's explanation of what has gone wrong. Ocol's teachers were like Lawino's teacher in the Evening Speaker's Class. If Ocol had run from them to the dance as Lawino did he would have learnt things that meant something to him:

> We joined the line of friends
> And danced among our age-mates
> And sang songs we understood,
> Relevant and meaningful songs,
> Songs about ourselves ... (p. 79)

Instead he went to school, where pupils shout:

> Meaninglessly in the evenings
> Like parrots ... (p. 75)

They do not understand what they shout and the teacher controls them only by his anger. It seems as if Ocol is still like a parrot, boasting in the market place and condemning everything that the white priests told him to condemn, instead of picking out the good from both African and European ways.

Song of Ocol again confirms Lawino's opinions. In Chapter 2 Ocol trots out for us the attitudes to Africa that he has swallowed whole from the missionaries:

> What is Africa
> To me?
> Blackness,
> Deep, deep fathomless
> Darkness ... (p. 125)

He goes on to tell us that Africans are ignorant, but stupidly content with their ignorant state. They are ruled by their fear of spirits and they have no technology. They are like children:

> Unweaned,
> Clinging to mother's milkless breasts ... (p. 126)

In Chapter 3, Ocol condemns all efforts to find reasons for pride in Africa's past. He would prefer to forget his past:

> Smash all these mirrors
> That I may not see
> The blackness of the past
> From which I came
> Reflected in them. (p. 129)

In other words, Ocol wants to deny his Africanness. These feelings wring from him the cry of anguish which ends Chapter 2:

> Mother, mother
> Why
> Why was I born
> Black? (p. 126)

Ocol's white teachers have made him think of his continent, his community, his family and himself as essentially evil. They have robbed him of all his self-respect. He is even ashamed of his own body. His bombastic arrogance and nervous violence of language are attempts to hide this shame. These are 'the winds' with which he has tried to 'blow away' the ways of his ancestors. He has failed to destroy their customs. But he has succeeded in breaking up his homestead, so that his wife mocks him publicly in song. He and his friends have succeeded in dividing his nation into bickering factions struggling for power while a discontented majority are permanently excluded from it. The beggar in Chapter 7 of *Song of Ocol* predicts revolution as a consequence of these divisions:

> A hunter
> Sat in the shadow
> Of a rock
> Rubbed two sticks
> A flash
> Flame
> Purified the land! (p. 145)

In the face of Lawino's mockery, Ocol blusters with rage. In the face of the beggar's threats, he is flippant and smug.

In Chapter 12, Lawino summarises what has happened to Ocol. Ocol has read many books '... among white men.' (p. 113). But the books have not helped him. Instead he has:

> ... lost his head
> In the forest of books. (p. 113)

And in the end the books have destroyed him:

> ... the reading
> Has killed my man,
> in the ways of his people
> He has become
> A stump. (p. 113)

Ocol still has the roles of husband and head of a household, but he is no longer able to perform them. Instead he has become:

> A dog of the white man! (p. 115)

The white man is his ultimate master, acting on him through his continuing cultural and economic influences. Ocol obeys his master's call and is pleased only by those things that belong to his master.

Ocol no longer owns anything. Everything he uses belong to his master:

> Aaa! A certain man
> Has no millet field
> He lives on borrowed foods
> He borrows the clothes he wears
> And the ideas in his head
> And his actions and behaviour
> Are to please somebody else
> Like a woman trying to please her husband!
> My husband has become a woman! (p. 116)

And many young men are the same. Lawino calls on her clansmen to weep for them because:

> Their manhood was finished
> In the classrooms
> Their testicles
> Were smashed
> With large books! (p. 117)

Here Lawino is mocking all those Ocols who are carrying the habit of slavish imitation of white men they learnt in the Mission School into every sphere of their lives in the new nations of Africa.

But this is not Lawino's final word. She thinks there is still hope for Ocol. Ocol only needs treatment to rid him of his disease. First Lawino recommends physical remedies (p. 117). Ocol's throat is blocked by the shame that has been choking him for so long:

> The shyness you ate in the church ... (p. 118)

It must be cleaned out by traditional foods and herbs. His ears are blocked by the things he has heard from priests and teachers. They must be cleaned. His eyes, behind his dark glasses, are blind to the things of his people. They must be opened. His tongue is dirty with the continuous flow of insults he has been pouring on his people. It must be cleaned.

When the physical remedies have been completed, Ocol will be ready

Introduction

for the real cure. He will be ready to regain his roots among his own
people. Lawino explains how he nearly lost those roots:

> When you took the axe
> And threatened to cut the Okango
> That grows on the ancestral shrine
> You were threatening
> To cut yourself loose,
> To be tossed by the winds
> This way and that way ... (pp. 119–20)

For this real cure, Ocol must beg forgiveness of all those he insulted.
But he must also seek the blessing of the elders and beg forgiveness
from the ancestors, because:

> ... when you insulted me
> Saying
> I was a mere village girl
> You were insulting your grandfathers
> And grandmothers ... (p. 119)

If he does all these things he will become a man again, the ancestors
will help him recover:

> Ask for a spear that you will trust
> One that does not bend easily
> Like the earth-worm
> Ask them to restore your manhood! (p. 119)

Lawino's final appeal concerns her domestic situation. She wants
things to be normal in the household again. She wants Ocol to behave
like her husband. And when he is recovered, if he only gives her:

> ... one chance ... (p. 120)

she is sure things will become normal. When his ears are unblocked
he will hear the beauty of her singing. When his blindness is cured,
he will see and appreciate her dancing:

> Let me dance before you
> My love,
> Let me show you
> The wealth in your house ... (p. 120)

When he is a man again, he will want her.

Ocol as Spokesman

If *Song of Ocol* is a reply to *Song of Lawino* then it is a bad one. Okot raises controversial issues in his poems, but he only puts one point of view in the controversy. I have already illustrated how many parts of *Song of Ocol* underline the points made in *Song of Lawino*. These two poems are not the thesis and antithesis of the argument, from which the reader can deduce a synthesis. Unlike some other African writers,[18] Okot doesn't consider a cultural synthesis to be the solution to Africa's problems. He wishes to borrow technology from Europe, but not culture. Okot has very little sympathy with Ocol, so he makes Ocol reply in a clumsy way. *Song of Ocol* does not fairly represent an alternative to Lawino's point of view.

This is why, if we think of these poems as separate works, *Song of Ocol* is much weaker than *Song of Lawino*. Another weakness is the lack of a clear situation in most of the poem. In *Song of Lawino*, Okot exploits the dramatic impact of the domestic conflict to express his more serious points about the future of Africa. Ocol is only concerned with his domestic situation for one chapter. At the end of the first chapter he sends Lawino away, and, except for one reference, in Chapter 8 forgets her. In Chapters 2 to 5 it is not clear who is being addressed. In Chapters 6 and 7, he is talking to his constituents, and in Chapter 9, he throws out a challenge to everybody in his nation with any position of importance.

This lack of a clear dramatic situation has reduced the popular impact of *Song of Ocol*. For a reader who has not read *Song of Lawino*, the widely differing issues raised in *Song of Ocol* are confusing. With the knowledge we bring to the poem from *Song of Lawino* the unity behind Ocol's differing concerns in the poem is clear. *Song of Lawino* considered alone is a coherent unit. The two poems considered together make a coherent unit. *Song of Ocol* considered alone is disjointed. It contains many excellent pieces of poetry expressing important ideas, but they pull in different directions.

Though Ocol does not effectively reply to most of the points Lawino raises, he does reply to some. In some places in the poem Ocol is the writer's spokesman. Okot's sympathies are mainly, but not entirely, with Lawino. Okot drinks beer and whisky as well as *kwete* and *waragi*. He usually wears trousers, though not a blanket suit. When he is ill he is prepared to use the white man's medicine to help him recover. He is anxious that Africa should have the benefits of technology. Through Lawino, he couldn't say these things. Through Ocol, he can and does.

In Chapter 3, Ocol briefly, but effectively, comments on traditional medicine. However foolish he might be in condemning all traditional remedies it is difficult not to share some of his horror at the scene he describes:

> That child lying
> On the earth
> Numb
> Bombs exploding in his head
> Blood boiling
> Heavy with malarial parasites
> Raging through his veins.
> The mad woman
> Spits on the palms
> Of his hands
> And on his feet
> Squirts beer
> On his face
> Spills chicken blood
> To cool him
> On his chest
> A gift of Death ... (p. 127)

Traditional remedies should have some place in Africa, but they cannot solve all her medical problems.

In Chapter 4 Ocol considers the position of women in traditional societies. It is interesting to compare his description of the walk from the well (p. 130) with Lawino's description of the walk to the well (p. 53). Lawino is happy with her traditional role, but she does have to work rather hard:

> Woman of Africa
> Sweeper
> Smearing floors and walls
> With cow dung and black soil
> Cook, *ayah*, the baby tied on your back,
> Vomiting,

> Washer of dishes,
> Planting, weeding, harvesting,
> Store-keeper, builder,
> Runner of errands,
> Cart, lorry
> Donkey ... (p. 133)

And in some ways here status is rather low:

> In Buganda
> They buy you
> With two pots
> Of beer,
> The Luo trade you
> For seven cows ... (p. 134)

If a little technology could reduce her work load, it would enable her to keep her beauty longer and she would have more time to dance before her husband.

In Chapter 5 Ocol makes fun of traditional concepts of manly behaviour. Ocol chooses a number of formerly powerful warrior communities of East Africa and challenges them to tell him what they have now gained from centuries of successful fighting:

> Survey your booty
> Study your empire
> Your gains ... (p. 136)

These nomadic groups are the ones who have suffered most through recent developments in East Africa. They are now trapped in areas of poor pasture with depleted stocks of cattle. Worst of all they suffer the humiliation of being objects of the curiosity of prying white people:

> Students of primitive man
> Big game hunters
> And tourists flocked in
> From all corners of the world,
> White women came to discover,
> To see with their naked eyes
> What manhood could be! (p. 136)

Ocol asks his questions in an unnecessarily offensive way, but he is throwing out to these people a challenge which they must in some way accept.

Introduction

The core of Ocol's speech in Chapter 9 is his expression of faith in the urban future of Africa, and in the foundations of that future laid by Europeans. Naively and improbably he promises to:

> ... erect monuments
> To the founders
> Of modern Africa:
> Leopold II of Belgium,
> Bismarck ... (p. 151)

But most of the speech is in the form of challenges to various people in positions of influence in Africa to explain the 'African foundation' (p. 150) of their activities. Here again Ocol is unwittingly speaking for Okot. Okot is mocking the borrowed plumes of all these dignitaries and challenging them to justify their borrowings.

Why should lawyers and bishops wear long robes as the English do? Why should the African legal system be based on English 'Law Reports'? Why should all the officials in local government take their names from English equivalents ('Mayors', 'Aldermen', 'Councillors', 'Town Clerks'). Okot's most serious challenge is to the 'scholar':

> Can you explain
> The African philosophy
> On which we are reconstructing
> Our new societies ... (p. 150)

Okot has made 'the foundation' on which he wishes to build African nations abundantly clear throughout this book. In these last pages he is challenging all concerned with nation building to reassess their own activities in the light of his ideas. If they don't accept the challenge, then, like Shaka, (p. 151), those like Nyerere and Senghor who are looking for an African mould for nation-building will be 'utterly defeated' by the continuing cultural influence of Europe on Africa.

* * *

I would like to thank J. P. Odoci for his help with the translations from Acoli.

G. A. Heron

Notes

1. For example: Dennis Osadebay, *Thank You Sons and Daughters of Britannia*; Thomas Mofolo, *The Traveller of the East* (London, 1934) and *Chaka: An Historical Romance* (London, 1931 and London, HEB [Heinemann Educational Books], AWS 229, 1981).
2. The best known of these poets are Leopold Senghor and Aime Cesaire but other poets from French speaking Africa associated themselves with this school of writing.
3. See Chinua Achebe, *Things Fall Apart* (London, HEB, AWS 1, 1962) and *Arrow of God* (London, HEB, AWS 16, 1965).
4. This story is retold by Taban lo Liyong in *Eating Chiefs* (London, HEB, AWS 74, 1970), p. 3.
5. Okot p'Bitek, *African Religions in Western Scholarship* (Nairobi, East African Literature Bureau, 1971; Towota, N.J., Rowman and Littlefield, 1972).
6. Ibid., Chapter 1, especially pp. 5 and 6.
7. *Wer pa Lawino* (Nairobi, East African Publishing House, 1969), p. 31. A fairly literal translation would read:
   > It happens in everything that they behave in the white people's way, for white people don't feel shame. They embrace other people's wives, like white people, they hold their chests close, like white people. You smoke cigarettes like white people, both men and women like white people. You kiss each other's lips like white people, you suck each other's mouths like white people, you lick up the spit of each other's mouths like white people, so that the mouths of the men are covered with the red paint of white people.
8. Ibid., p. 26.
9. From Okot p'Bitek's *The Horn of My Love* (London, HEB, AWS 147, 1974).
10. Taban lo Liyong, *The Last Word* (Nairobi, EAPH [East African Publishing House], 1969), 'Lawino is Unedu', p. 141.
11. Ibid., p. 140.
12. *Wer pa Lawino*, op. cit., p. 38.
13. In the Kyambogo T.T. College magazine *Nanga*, Vol. 2, No. 3, May 1970.
14. lo Liyong, op. cit., p. 141.
15. p'Bitek, *African Religions in Western Scholarship*, op. cit., p. 22.
16. Ibid., p. 117.
17. See John Mbiti, *African Religions and Philosophy* (London, HEB, 1969), p. 10:
    > African religions and philosophy have been subjected to a great deal of misinterpretation, misrepresentation and misunderstanding. They have been despised, mocked and dismissed as primitive and underdeveloped ... In missionary circles they have been condemned as superstition, satanic, devilish and hellish. In spite of all these attacks, traditional religions have survived, they dominate the background of African peoples, and must be reckoned with even in the middle of modern changes.
18. lo Liyong, op. cit., p. 206:
    > African culture is to be a synthesis and a metamorphosis—the order of things to come. It assimilates and it disseminates. It picks, it grabs, it carries on ... A racially and culturally mixed person is the universal man; all is in him; he identifies with all; he is kith and kin to all other Homo Sapiens.

Song of Lawino

I

My Husband's Tongue is Bitter

Husband, now you despise me
Now you treat me with spite
And say I have inherited the
    stupidity of my aunt;
Son of the Chief,
Now you compare me
With the rubbish in the rubbish
    pit,
You say you no longer want me
Because I am like the things left
    behind
In the deserted homestead.
You insult me
You laugh at me
You say I do not know the letter
    A
Because I have not been to school
And I have not been baptized

You compare me with a little dog,
A puppy.

My friend, age-mate of my
    brother,
Take care,

Take care of your tongue,
Be careful what your lips say.

First take a deep look, brother,
You are now a man
You are not a dead fruit!
To behave like a child does not
    befit you!

Listen Ocol, you are the son of a
    Chief,
Leave foolish behaviour to little
    children,
It is not right that you should
    be laughed at in a song!
Songs about you should be songs
    of praise!

Stop despising people
As if you were a little foolish man,
Stop treating me like salt-less
    ash*
Become barren of insults and
    stupidity;

* Salt is extracted from the ash of certain plants, and also from the ash of the dung
of domestic animals. The ash is put in a container with small holes in its bottom,
water is then poured on the ash, and the salty water is collected in another container
placed below. The useless saltless ash is then thrown on the pathway and people tread
on it.

Who has ever uprooted the
  Pumpkin?

★

My clansmen, I cry
Listen to my voice:
The insults of my man
Are painful beyond bearing.

My husband abuses me together
  with my parents;
He says terrible things about my
  mother
And I am so ashamed!

He abuses me in English
And he is so arrogant.

He says I am rubbish,
He no longer wants me!
In cruel jokes, he laughs at me,
He says I am primitive
Because I cannot play the guitar,
He says my eyes are dead
And I cannot read,
He says my ears are blocked
And cannot hear a single foreign
  word,
That I cannot count the coins.

He says I am like sheep,
The fool.

Ocol treats me
As if I am no longer a person,
He says I am silly
Like the *ojuu* insects that sit on
  the beer pot.

My husband treats me roughly.
The insults!
Words cut more painfully than
  sticks!
He says my mother is a witch,
That my clansmen are fools
Because they eat rats,
He says we are all Kaffirs.
We do not know the ways of
  God,
We sit in deep darkness
And do not know the Gospel,
He says my mother hides her
  charms
In her necklace
And that we are all sorcerers.

My husband's tongue
Is bitter like the roots of the
  lyonno lily,
It is hot like the penis of the bee,
Like the sting of the *kalang*!
Ocol's tongue is fierce like the
  arrow of the scorpion,
Deadly like the spear of the
  buffalo-hornet.
It is ferocious
Like the poison of a barren
  woman
And corrosive like the juice of
  the gourd.

My husband pours scorn
On Black People,
He behaves like a hen
That eats its own eggs
A hen that should be imprisoned
  under a basket.

His eyes grow large
Deep black eyes
Ocol's eyes resemble those of
  the Nile Perch!
He becomes fierce
Like a lioness with cubs,
He begins to behave like a
  mad hyena.

He says Black People are
  primitive
And their ways are utterly
  harmful,
Their dances are mortal sins
They are ignorant, poor and
  diseased!

Ocol says he is a modern man,
A progressive and civilized man,

He says he has read extensively
  and widely
And he can no longer live with
  a thing like me
Who cannot distinguish between
  good and bad.

He says I am just a village
  woman,
I am of the old type,
And no longer attractive.

He says I am blocking his
  progress,
My head, he says,
Is as big as that of an elephant
But it is only bones,
There is no brain in it,
He says I am only wasting his
  time.

2

The Woman With Whom I Share My Husband

Ocol rejects the old type.
He is in love with a modern
  woman,
He is in love with a beautiful
  girl
Who speaks English.

But only recently
We would sit close together,
  touching each other!

Only recently I would play
On my bow-harp
Singing praises to my beloved.
Only recently he promised
That he trusted me completely.
I used to admire him speaking
  in English.

★

Ocol is no longer in love with
  the old type;
He is in love with a modern girl.
The name of the beautiful one
Is Clementine.

Brother, when you see
  Clementine!
The beautiful one aspires
To look like a white woman;

Her lips are red-hot
Like glowing charcoal,
She resembles the wild cat
That has dipped its mouth in
  blood,
Her mouth is like raw yaws
It looks like an open ulcer,
Like the mouth of a field!
Tina dusts powder on her face
And it looks so pale;
She resembles the wizard
Getting ready for the midnight
  dance.

She dusts the ash-dirt all over
  her face
And when little sweat
Begins to appear on her body
She looks like the guinea fowl!

The smell of carbolic soap
Makes me sick,
And the smell of powder
Provokes the ghosts in my head;
It is then necessary to fetch a goat
From my mother's brother.
The sacrifice over

The ghost-dance drum must
  sound
The ghost be laid
And my peace restored.

I do not like dusting myself
  with powder:
The thing is good on pink skin
Because it is already pale,
But when a black woman has
  used it
She looks as if she has
  dysentery;
Tina looks sickly
And she is slow moving,
She is a piteous sight.

Some medicine has eaten up
  Tina's face;
The skin on her face is gone
And it is all raw and red,
The face of the beautiful one
Is tender like the skin of a newly
  born baby!

And she believes
That this is beautiful
Because it resembles the face of
  a white woman!
Her body resembles
The ugly coat of the hyena;
Her neck and arms
Have real human skins!
She looks as if she has been
  struck
By lightning;

Or burnt like the kongoni
In a fire hunt.

She dusts the ash-dirt all over her face
And when little sweat
Begins to appear on her body
She looks like the guinea fowl!

And her lips look like bleeding,
Her hair is long
Her head is huge like that of
the owl,
She looks like a witch,
Like someone who has lost her
head
And should be taken
To the clan shrine!
Her neck is rope-like,
Thin, long and skinny
And her face sickly pale.

★

Forgive me, brother,
Do not think I am insulting
The woman with whom I share
my husband!
Do not think my tongue
Is being sharpened by jealousy.
It is the sight of Tina
That provokes sympathy from
my heart.

I do not deny
I am a little jealous.
It is no good lying,
We all suffer from a little jealousy.
It catches you unawares
Like the ghosts that bring fevers;
It surprises people
Like earth tremors:
But when you see the beautiful
woman
With whom I share my husband
You feel a little pity for her!

Her breasts are completely
shrivelled up,

They are all folded dry skins,
They have made nests of cotton
wool
And she folds the bits of
cow-hide
In the nests
And call them breasts!

O! my clansmen
How aged modern women
Pretend to be young girls!

They mould the tips of the
cotton nests
So that they are sharp
And with these they prick
The chests of their men!
And the men believe
They are holding the waists
Of young girls that have just
shot up!
The modern type sleep with
their nests
Tied firmly on their chests.
How many kids
Has this woman sucked?
The empty bags on her chest
Are completely flattened, dried.

Perhaps she has aborted many!
Perhaps she has thrown her twins
In the pit latrine!
Is it the vengeance ghosts
Of the many smashed eggs
That have captured her head?
How young is this age-mate of
my mother?

★

The woman with whom I share
   my husband
Walks as if her shadow
Has been captured,
You can never hear
Her footsteps;

She looks as if
She has been ill for a long time!
Actually she is starving
She does not eat,
She says she fears getting fat,
That the doctor has prevented
   her
From eating,
She says a beautiful woman
Must be slim like a white
   woman;

And when she walks
You hear her bones rattling,
Her waist resembles that of the
   hornet.
The beautiful one is dead dry
Like a stump,
She is meatless
Like a shell
On a dry river bed.

★

But my husband despises me,
He laughs at me,
He says he is too good
To be my husband.

Ocol says he is not
The age-mate of my
   grandfather

To live with someone like me
Who has not been to school.

He speaks with arrogance,
Ocol is bold;
He says these things in broad
   daylight.
He says there is no difference
Between me and my
   grandmother
Who covers herself with animal
   skins.

★

I am not unfair to my husband,
I do not complain
Because he wants another woman
Whether she is young or aged!
Who has ever prevented men
From wanting women?

Who has discovered the
   medicine for thirst?
The medicines for hunger
And anger and enmity
Who has discovered them?
In the dry season the sun shines
And rain falls in the wet season.
Women hunt for men
And men want women!
When I have another woman
With whom I share my husband,
I am glad
A woman who is jealous
Of another, with whom she
   shares a man,
Is jealous because she is slow,
Lazy and shy,

Because she is cold, weak, clumsy!
The competition for a man's love
Is fought at the cooking place
When he returns from the field
Or from the hunt,

You win him with a hot bath
And sour porridge.
The wife who brings her meal
     first
Whose food is good to eat,
Whose dish is hot
Whose face is bright
And whose heart is clean
And whose eyes are dark
Like the shadows:

The wife who jokes freely
Who eats in the open
Not in the bed room,
One who is not dull
Like stale beer,
Such is the woman who becomes
The headdress keeper.

I do not block my husband's path
From his new wife.
If he likes, let him build for her
An iron roofed house on the hill!
I do not complain,
My grass thatched house is
     enough for me.

I am not angry
With the woman with whom

I share my husband,
I do not fear to compete with her.

All I ask
Is that my husband should stop
     the insults,
My husband should refrain
From heaping abuses on my head.
He should stop being half-crazy,
And saying terrible things about
     my mother
Listen Ocol, my old friend,
The ways of your ancestors
Are good,
Their customs are solid
And not hollow
They are not thin, not easily
     breakable
They cannot be blown away
By the winds
Because their roots reach deep
     into the soil.

I do not understand
The ways of foreigners
But I do not despise their
     customs.
Why should you despise yours?

Listen, my husband,
You are the son of a Chief.
The pumpkin in the old
     homestead
Must not be uprooted!

3

I Do Not Know the Dances of White People

It is true
I am ignorant of the dances of
    foreigners
And how they dress
I do not know.
Their games
I cannot play,
I only know the dances of our
    people.

I cannot dance the rumba,
My mother taught me
The beautiful dances of Acoli.
I do not know the dances of
    White People.
I will not deceive you,
I cannot dance the samba!
You once saw me at the *orak*
    dance
The dance for youths
The dance of our People.

When the drums are throbbing
And the black youths
Have raised much dust
You dance with vigour and
    health
You dance naughtily with pride
You dance with spirit,
You compete, you insult, you
    provoke

You challenge all!
And the eyes of the young men
    become red!

The son of a man
And the daughter of a man
Shine forth in the arena.
Slave boys and girls
Dance differently from true-
    borns.

You dance with confidence
And you sing
Provocative songs,
Insulting and abusive songs
Songs of praise
Sad songs of broken loves
Songs about shortage of cattle.
Most of the songs make
    someone angry.

You do not come to the arena
    drunk,
But when another youth hits
    you
You take up the challenge
As a man,

And when a girl knocks you
You strike back,

A man's manliness is seen in
    the arena,
No one touches another's
    testicles.

A girl whose waist is stiff
Is a clumsy girl
That is the lazy girl
Who fears grinding the *kabir*
    millet.

You adorn yourself in Acoli
    costumes
You tie *lacucuku* rattles
Or bells on your legs.
You wear bead-skirts or string
    skirts
Or a tiny piece of cloth
And a ten-stringed bead
Around your waist;
Bangles on your arms,
And giraffe-tail necklaces on
    your tall neck.

A young man wears the *odye*
    and *lacomi*,
He puts his lover's beads
On his neck,
Beautiful white feathers on his
    head,
He blows his horn
And other young men feel
    jealous of him.

It is danced in broad daylight
In the open,
You cannot hide anything,
Bad stomachs that have swollen
    up,

Skin diseases on the buttocks
Small breasts that have just
    emerged,
And large ones full of boiling
    milk,
Are clearly seen in the arena,
Breasts that are tired
And are about to fall,

Weak and bony chests of
    weaklings
Strong lion chests
Large scars on the thighs
Beautiful tattoos below the belly
    button
Tattoos that have become sores
    on the chest;

All parts of the body
Are shown in the arena!
Health and liveliness
Are shown in the arena!

When the daughter of the Bull
Enters the arena
She does not stand here
Like stale beer that does not
    sell,
She jumps here
She jumps there.
When you touch her
She says 'Don't touch me!'

The tattoos on her chest
Are like palm fruits,
The tattoos on her back
Are like stars on a black night;
Her eyes sparkle like the
    fireflies,

Her breasts are ripe
Like the full moon.
When the age-mate of her
    brother sees them,
When, by accident,
The eyes of her lover
Fall on her breasts
Do you think the young man
    sleeps?
Do you know what fire eats his
    inside?

★

It is true, Ocol
I cannot dance the ballroom
    dance.
Being held so tightly
I feel ashamed,
Being held so tightly in public
I cannot do it,
It looks shameful to me!

They come to the dance dead
    drunk
They drink white men's drinks
As well as *waragi*.
They close their eyes,
And they do not sing as they
    dance,
They dance silently like wizards.

Each man has a woman
Although she is not his wife,
They dance inside a house
And there is no light.
Shamelessly, they hold each
    other
Tightly, tightly,

They cannot breathe!

Women lie on the chests of men
They prick the chests of their
    men
With their breasts
They prick the chests of their
    men
With the cotton nests
On their chests.

★

You kiss her on the cheek
As white people do,
You kiss her open-sore lips
As white people do,
You suck slimy saliva
From each other's mouths
As white people do.

And the lips of the men become
    bloody
With blood dripping from the
    red-hot lips;
Their teeth look
As if they have been boxed in
    the mouth.

Women throw their arms
Around the necks of their
    partners
And put their cheeks
On the cheeks of their men.
Men hold the waists of the
    women
Tightly, tightly . . .

And as they dance
Knees touch knees;

And when the music has stopped
Men put their hands in the
    trouser-pockets.

There is no respect for relatives:
Girls hold their fathers,
Boys hold their sisters close,
They dance even with their
    mothers.
Modern girls are fierce
Like Labeja, the *Jok* of *Alero**,
That captures even the heads of
    nephews,
They coil around their nephews
And lie on the chests of their
    uncles
And prick the chests of their
    brothers
With their breasts.

And they dress up like white
    men,
As if they are in the white
    man's country.
At the height of the hot season
The progressive and civilised
    ones
Put on blanket suits
And woollen socks from Europe,
Long under-pants
And woollen vests,
White shirts;
They wear dark glasses
And neck-ties from Europe.
Their waterlogged suits
Drip like the tears

Of the *kituba* tree
After a heavy storm.

You smoke cigars
Like white men,
Women smoke cigarettes
Like white women,
And sip some poisons from the
    glasses.

It is hot inside the house
It is hot like inside a cave
Like inside a hyena's den!
And the women move like fish
That have been poisoned,
They stagger
They fall face upwards
Like fish that are dead drunk
With *lugoro* or *ober*;
Like small fish out of water.

The smoke of the tobacco
The smoke of the cigars
And the cigarettes
And the smoke of the candles
Used for counting the coins,
The smoke in the house
Is like cumulus clouds.

The evaporating vapour
From the many drinks,
The steaming sweat
The hot wet breaths
Of the numerous people,

---

*A chiefdom divinity. Other chiefdom divinities possess only persons within the
chiefdom. But Labeja possesses even outsiders, e.g. a mother's brother.

The coughs and saliva
Squirted by sneezing drunken
   sick,
The many brands
Of winds broken,
Humid winds broken by men
   and women
Producing various types of
   smells,
The dust
The evaporating piss . . .
The air is heavy like the
   hammer.

The stench from the urinal is
   thick!
It hits your nose
Like a blow,
Like a horn of a bull rhino!
You choke
Your throat pains sharply
You get out quick
And shout a curse!

You meet a big woman
She staggers towards you
And leans on the wall
And before she has untied her
   dress
She is already pissing;
She forces out the urine
As if she has syphilis.

★

The stench from the latrine
Knocks you down, from afar!
You enter;
It is as if you have entered

Into a lion's mouth.
The smell of Jeyes
And the smell of dung
Rise to the roof.

The entire floor
Is covered with human dung
All the tribes of human dung!
Dry dungs and dysentery
Old dungs and fresh dungs

Young ones that are still
   steaming,
Short thick dungs
Sitting like hills,
Snake-like dungs
Coiled up like pythons.
Little ones just squatting there,
Big ones lying on their sides
Like tree trunks.

Some dungs are red like ochre
Others are yellow
Like the ripe mango,
Like inside a ripe pawpaw.
Others are black like soil,
Like the soil we use
For smearing the floor.
Some dungs are of mixed colours!

Vomit and urine flow by
And on the walls
They clean their anus.
And there are writings
On the walls
Cut with knives.

★

46

My husband laughs at me
Because I cannot dance white
   men's dances;
He despises Acoli dances
He nurses stupid ideas
That the dances of his People
Are sinful,
That they are mortal sins.

I am completely ignorant
Of the dances of foreigners
And I do not like it.
Holding each other
Tightly, tightly
In public,

I cannot.
I am ashamed.
Dancing without a song
Dancing silently like wizards,
Without respect, drunk ...

If someone tries
To force me to dance this
   dance
I feel like hanging myself
Feet first!

I wish I could become
A meteorite
And I would know
Where to fall!

4

My Name Blew
Like a Horn Among the Payira

I was made chief of girls
Because I was lively,
I was bright,
I was not clumsy or untidy
I was not dull,
I was not heavy and slow.

I did not grow up a fool
I am not cold
I am not shy
My skin is smooth
It still shines smoothly in the
   moonlight.

When Ocol was wooing me
My breasts were erect.
And they shook
As I walked briskly,
And as I walked
I threw my long neck
This way and that way
Like the flower of the *lyonno* lily
Waving in a gentle breeze.

And my brothers called me
   Nya-Dyang
For my breasts shook

And beckoned the cattle,
And they sang silently:

Father prepare the kraal,
Father prepare the kraal,
The cattle are coming.

I was the Leader of the girls
And my name blew
Like a horn
Among the Payira.
And I played on my bow harp
And praised my love.

Ocol, my husband,
My friend,
What are you talking?
You saw me when I was young.
In my mother's house
This man crawled on the floor!
The son of the Bull wept
For me with tears,
Like a hungry child
Whose mother has stayed long
In the simsim field!

Every night he came
To my father's homestead,
He never missed one night
Even after he had been beaten
By my brothers.

You loved my giraffe-tail bangles,
My father bought them for me
From the Hills in the East.

The roof of my mother's house
Was beautifully laced
With elephant grass;

My father built it
With the skill of the Acoli.

You admired my sister's
Colourful ten-stringed lion
beads;
My mother threaded them
And arranged them with care.

You trembled
When you saw the tattoos
On my breasts
And the tattoos below my belly
button;
And you were very fond
Of the gap in my teeth!
My man, what are you talking?
My clansmen, I ask you:
What has become of my
husband?
Is he suffering from boils?
Is it ripe now?
Should they open it
So that the pus may flow out?

★

I was chief of youths
Because of my good manners,
Because my waist was soft.
I sang sweetly
When I was grinding millet
Or on the way to the well,
Nobody's voice was sweeter
than mine!
And in the arena
I sang the solos
Loud and clear
Like the *ogilo* bird
At sunset.

Now, Ocol says
I am a mere dog
A puppy,
A little puppy
Suffering from skin diseases.

Ocol says
He does not love me any more
Because I cannot play the guitar
And I do not like their stupid
    dance,
Because I despise the songs
They play at the ballroom
    dance
And I do not follow the steps
    of foreign songs
On the gramophone records.
And I cannot tune the radio
Because I do not hear
Swahili or Luganda.

What is all this?

My husband refuses
To listen to me,
He refuses to give me a chance.
My husband has blocked up my
    path completely.

He has put up a road block
But has not told me why.
He just shouts
Like house-flies
Settling on top of excrement
When disturbed!

My husband says
He no longer wants a woman
With a gap in her teeth,
He is in love
With a woman
Whose teeth fill her mouth
    completely
Like the teeth of war-captives
    and slaves.

★

Like beggars
You take up white men's
    adornments,
Like slaves or war captives
You take up white men's ways.
Didn't the Acoli have
    adornments?
Didn't Black People have their
    ways?

Like drunken men
You stagger to white men's
    games,
You stagger to white men's
    amusements.

Is *lawala* not a game?
Is *cooro** not a game?
Didn't your people have
    amusements?
Like halfwits
You turn to white men's dances,
You turn to musical instruments
    of foreigners

* *Lawala* is a hunting game. *Cooro* is a board
  game.

49

As if you have no dances;
As if you have no instruments!

And you cannot sing one song
You cannot sing a solo
In the arena.
You cannot beat rhythm on the
    half-gourd
Or shake the rattle-gourd
To the rhythm of the *orak*
    dance!
And there is not a single *bwola*
    song
That you can dance,
You do not play the drum
Or do the mock-fight;
At the funeral dance
Or at the war dance
You cannot wield the shield!

And so you turn
To the dances of white people,

Ignorance and shame provoke
    you
To turn to foreign things!

Perhaps you are covering up
Your bony hips and chest
And the large scar on your
    thigh
And the scabies on your buttocks;

You are hiding
Under the blanket suit
Your sick stomach
That has swollen up
Like that of a pregnant goat.

And the dark glasses
Shield the rotting skin around
    your eyes
From the house-flies,
And cover up
The husks of the exploded eye
    balls.

5

The Graceful Giraffe Cannot Become a Monkey

My husband tells me
I have no ideas
Of modern beauty.
He says
I have stuck
To old fashioned hair styles.

He says
I am stupid and very backward,
That my hair style
Makes him sick
Because I am dirty.

It is true
I cannot do my hair
As white women do.

Listen,
My father comes from Payira,
My mother is a woman of Koc!
I am a true Acoli
I am not a half-caste
I am not a slave girl;
My father was not brought
   home
Be the spear
My mother was not exchanged
For a basket of millet.

Ask me what beauty is
To the Acoli
And I will tell you;
I will show it to you
If you give me a chance!

You once saw me,
You saw my hair style
And you admired it,
And the boys loved it.
At the arena
Boys surrounded me
And fought for me.

My mother taught me
Acoli hair fashions;
Which fits the kind
Of hair of the Acoli,
And the occasion.

Listen,
Ostrich plumes differ
From chicken feathers,

A monkey's tail
Is different from that of the
   giraffe,
The crocodile's skin
Is not like the guinea fowl's,
And the hippo is naked, and
   hairless.

The hair of the Acoli
Is different from that of the
   Arabs;
The Indians' hair
Resembles the tail of the horse;
It is like sisal strings
And needs to be cut
With scissors.
It is black,
And is different from that of
   white women.

A white woman's hair
Is soft like silk;
It is light
And brownish like
That of the brown monkey,
And is very different from mine.
A black woman's hair
Is thick and curly;
It is true
Ring-worm sometimes eats up
A little girl's hair
And this is terrible;
But when hot porridge
Is put on the head
And the dance is held
Under the sausage-fruit tree
And the youths have sung

   You, Ring-worm,

51

*Who is eating Duka's hair
Here is your porridge,*

Then the girl's hair
Begins to grow again
And the girl is pleased.

★

No-one, except wizards
And women who poison others
Leaves her hair untrimmed!
And the men
Do not leave their chins
To grow bushy
Like the lion's neck,
Like the chin
Of a billy goat,
So that they look
Like wild beasts.
They put hot ash
On the hair
Below the belly button
And pluck it up,
And they pluck the hair on their
    face
And the hair of the armpits.

When death has occurred
Women leave their hair
    uncombed!
They remove all beads
And necklaces,
Because they are mourning
Because of sorrows.
The woman who adorns herself
When others are wailing

Is the killer!
She comes to the funeral
To congratulate herself.

When you go to dance
You adorn yourself for the
    dance,
If your string-skirt
Is ochre-red
You do your hair
With ochre,
And you smear your body
With red oil
And you are beautifully red all
    over!
If you put on a black string-skirt
You do your hair with *akuku*
Your body shines with simsim oil
And the tattoos on your chest
And on your back
Glitter in the evening sun.
And the healthy sweat
On your bosom
Is like the glassy fruits of *ocuga*.

Young girls
Whose breasts are just emerging
Smear *shea* butter on their
    bodies,
The beautiful oil from Labwor-
    omor.

The aroma is wonderful
And their white teeth sparkle
As they sing
And dance fast
Among the dancers
Like small fish
In a shallow stream.

Butter from cows' milk
Or the fat from edible rats
Is cooked together with *lakura*
Or *atika*;
You smear it on your body
    today
And the aroma
Lasts until the next day.

And when you balance on your
    head
A beautiful water pot
Or a new basket
Or a long-necked jar
Full of honey,
Your long neck
Resembles the *alwiri* spear.

And as you walk along the
    pathway
On both sides
The *obiya* grasses are flowering
And the *pollok* blossoms
And the wild white lilies
Are shouting silently
To the bees and butterflies!

And as the fragrance
Of the ripe wild berries
Hooks the insects and little
    birds,
As the fishermen hook the fish
And pull them up mercilessly,

The young men
From the surrounding villages,
And from across many streams,
They come from beyond the hills
And the wide plains,

They surround you
And bite off their ears
Like jackals.

And when you go
To the well
Or into the freshly burnt
    woodlands
To collect the red *oceyu*,
Or to cut *oduggu* shrubs,
You find them
Lurking in the shades
Like the leopardess with cubs.

★

Ocol tells me
That I like dirt.
He says
Shea butter causes
Skin diseases.

He says, Acoli adornments
Are old fashioned and
    unhealthy.
He says I soil his white shirt
If I touch him,
My husband treats me
As if I am suffering from
The 'Don't touch me' disease!

He says that I make his bed-
    sheets dirty
And his bed smelly.
Ocol says
I look extremely ugly
When I am fully adorned
For the dance!

53

When I walk past my husband
He hisses like a wounded *ororo*
   snake
Choking with vengeance.
He has vowed
That he will never touch
My hands again.
My husband
Is in love with Tina
The woman with the large head;
Ocol dies for Clementine
Ocol never sleeps
For the beautiful one
Who has read!

When the beautiful one
With whom I share my husband
Returns from cooking her hair
She resembles
A chicken
That has fallen into a pond;
Her hair looks
Like the python's discarded skin.

They cook their hair
With hot iron
And pull it hard
So that it may grow long.
Then they rope the hair
On wooden pens
Like a billy goat
Brought for the sacrifice
Struggling to free itself.

They fry their hair
In boiling oil
As if it were locusts,
And the hair sizzles
It cries aloud in sharp pain

As it is pulled and stretched.
And the vigorous and healthy
   hair
Curly, springy and thick
That glistens in the sunshine
Is left listless and dead
Like the elephant grass
Scorched brown by the fierce
February sun.
It lies lifeless
Like the sad and dying banana
   leaves
On a hot and windless
   afternoon.

The beautiful woman
With whom I share my husband
Smears black shoe polish
On her hair
To blacken it
And to make it shine,
She washes her hair
With black ink;

But the thick undergrowth
Rejects the shoe polish
And the ink
And it remains untouched
Yellowish, greyish
Like the hair of the grey
   monkey.

★

There is much water
In my husband's house
Cold water and hot water.
You twist a cross–like handle
And water gushes out

54

Hot and steaming
Like the urine
Of the elephant.

You twist another cross-like
    handle;
It is cold water,
Clean like the cooling fresh
    waters
From the streams
Of Lututuru hills.

But the woman
With whom I share my husband
Does not wash her head;
The head of the beautiful one
Smells like rats
That have fallen into the
    fireplace.

And she uses
Powerful perfumes
To overcome the strange smells,
As they treat a pregnant coffin!
And the different smells
Wrestle with one another
And the smell of the shoe polish
Mingles with them.

Clementine has many
    headkerchiefs,
Beautiful headkerchiefs of many
    colours.
She ties one on her head
And it covers up
The rot inside;

She ties the knot
On her forehead

And arranges the edges
With much care
So that it covers
Her ears
As well as the bold forehead
That jumps sparks
When lightning has splashed,
And hurls back sunlight
More powerfully than a mirror!

Sometimes she wears
The hair of some dead woman
Of some white woman
Who died long ago
And she goes with it
To the dance!
What witchcraft!

Shamelessly, she dances
Holding the shoulder of my
    husband,
The hair of a dead woman
On her head
The body of the dead woman
Decaying in the tomb!

One night
The ghost of the dead woman
Pulled away her hair
From the head of the wizard

And the beautiful one
Fell down
And shook with shame
She shook
As if the angry ghost
Of the white woman
Had entered her head.

★

Ocol, my friend
Look at my skin
It is smooth and black.
And my boy friend
Who plays the *nanga*
Sings praises to it.

I am proud of the hair
With which I was born
And as no white woman
Wishes to do her hair
Like mine,
Because she is proud
Of the hair with which she was
    born,

I have no wish
To look like a white woman.

No leopard
Would change into a hyena,
And the crested crane
Would hate to be changed
Into the bold-headed,
Dung-eating vulture,
The long-necked and graceful
    giraffe
Cannot become a monkey.

Let no one
Uproot the Pumpkin.

6

The Mother Stone Has a Hollow Stomach

My husband says
He rejects me
Because I do not appreciate
White men's foods,
And that I do not know
How to hold
The spoon and the fork.

He is angry with me
Because I do not know
How to cook
As white women do
And I refuse
To eat chicken

And to drink raw eggs
As white women do

He says
He is ashamed of me
Because when he opens
The tin of lobster
I feel terribly sick,
Or when he relates
How, when he was in the white
    men's country
They ate frogs and shells
And tortoise and snakes
My stomach rebels

56

And throws its contents out
Through my mouth.

He complains endlessly,
He says
Has I been to school
I would have learnt
How to use
White men's cooking stoves.

I confess,
I do not deny!
I do not know
How to cook like a white
  woman.

I cannot use the primus stove
I do not know
How to light it,
And when it gets blocked
How can I prick it?
The thing roars
Like a male lion,
It frightens me!

They say
It once burst
And the flame burnt
A goat to death!

I really hate
The charcoal stove!
Your hand is always
Charcoal-dirty
And anything you touch

Is blackened;
And your finger nails
Resemble those of the poison
  woman.
It is so difficult to start:

You wait for the winds
To blow,
But whenever you are in a hurry
The winds go off to visit
Their mothers-in-law.

The electric fire kills people.
They say
It is lightning,
They say
The white man has trapped
And caught the Rain-Cock*
And imprisoned it
In a heavy steel house.

The wonders of the white men
Are many!
They leave me speechless!

They say
When the Rain-Cock
Opens its wings
The blinding light
And the deadly fire
Flow through the wires
And lighten the streets
And the houses;
And the fire
Goes into the electric stove.

* It is believed that lightning and thunder are caused by a giant reddish-brown bird that
is almost identical with the domestic fowl. When it opens its wings lightning flashes
and thunder is caused when its strikes with its powerful bolt.

If you touch it
It runs through you
And cuts the heart string
As they cut the umbilical cord,
And you stand there, dead,
A standing corpse!

I am terribly afraid
Of the electric stove,
And I do not like using it
Because you stand up
When you cook.
Who ever cooked standing up?
And the stove
Has many eyes.
I do not know
Which eye to prick
So that the stove
May vomit fire
And I cannot tell
Which eye to prick
So that fire is vomited
In one and not in another plate.

And I am afraid
That I may touch
The deadly tongue
Of the Rain-Cock.

O! I do not like
Using the electric stove,
I cannot cook anything well
When you give me
The Rain-Cock stove.

★

The white man's stoves
Are good for cooking

White men's food:
For cooking the tasteless
Bloodless meat of cows
That were killed many years ago
And left in the ice
To rot!
For frying an egg
Which when ready
Is slimy like mucus,

For boiling hairy chicken
In saltless water.
You think you are chewing
   paper!
And the bones of the leg
Contain only clotted blood
And when you bite
It makes no crackling sound,
It tastes like earth!

The white man's stoves
Are for boiling cabbages
And for baking the light spongy
   thing
They call bread.

They are for warming up
Tinned beef, tinned fish,
Tinned frogs, tinned snakes,
Tinned peas, tinned beans,
Big broad beans
Tasteless like the *cooro*!

They are for preparing
Foods for the toothless,
For infants and invalids.
It is for making tea or coffee!

You use the saucepan
And the frying pan
And other flat-bottomed things,
Because the stoves are flat
Like the face of the drum.

The earthen vegetable pot
Cannot sit on it,
There are no stones
On which to place
The pot for making millet
    bread.

★

Come, brother,
Come into my mother's house!
Pause a bit by the door,
Let me show you
My mother's house.

Look,
Straight before you
Is the central pole.
That shiny stool
At the foot of the pole
Is my father's revered stool.

Further on
The rows of pots
Placed one on top of the other
Are the stores
And cupboards.
Millet flour, dried carcasses
Of various animals,
Beans, peas,
Fish, dried cucumber ...

Look up to the roof,

You see the hangings?
The string nets
Are called *cel*.
The beautiful long-necked jar
On your left
Is full of honey.
That earthen dish
Contains simsim paste;
And that grass pocket
Just above the fireplace
Contains dried white ants.

Here on your left
Are the grinding stones:
The big one
Ashen and dusty
And her daughter
Sitting in her belly
Are the destroyers of millet
Mixed with cassava
And sorghum.

The mother stone
Has a hollow stomach,
A strange woman
She never gets pregnant;
And her daughter
Never gets fatter
She gets smaller and smaller
Until she is finished.

Do you know
Why the knees
Of millet-eaters
Are tough?
Tougher than the knees
Of the people who drink
    bananas!
Where do you think

The stone powder
From the grinding stone goes?

On this stone
They also grind
Dried beans and peas.
The sister stone,
The smaller one,
Clean and beautifully oiled
Like a girl
Ready for the *jok* dance,
Is the simsim grinding stone.

And when my sister
Is grinding simsim
Mixed with groundnuts
And I am grinding
Millet mixed with sorghum
You hear the song of the stones
You hear the song of the grains
And the seeds
And above all these
The beautiful duet
By Lawino and her sister.

O how I miss my sister
And how I miss the singing
While grinding millet in my
    mother's house!

On your left
Above the grinding stone
Stacked right to the roof
Is the firewood.
If you ask me
About firewood

I can describe them to you in
    detail
I know their names
And their leaves
And seeds and barks.

Oywelo and *lucoro* and *kituba*
Are no use as firewood,
They burn like paper
They are like pawpaw
Their fires are cold
Like the firefly's fire.

Labwori is alright
If it is perfectly dry.
But if it is still green
The smoke it produces
Is like a spear!
It is useful for
Chasing men from the hut
Men who sit too close
To the cooking place
Their eyes fixed into the pot!
*Odure** who does not
Listen when others sing

    Odure, *come out*
    From the kitchen.
    Fire from the stove
    Will burn your penis!

Opok is easy
To split with the axe;
Yaa burns gently
It burns like oil;
Poi is no use for firewood,

* *Odure* is the nickname for small boys who are fond of sitting in the house when mother is cooking. It was derived from a small boy of that name whose penis was burnt by the fire from the stove.

It is rock;
It is useful only
As a walking staff
For the aged.

★

On the far right
Is the cooking place.
The fireplace in my mother's
    house
Is dug into the earth.
The wife of my mother's brother
Has the Lango type,
Three mounds of clay
Shaped like youthful breasts full
    of milk
Stand together like
Three loving sisters.

I do not know
How to use foreign stoves,
My mother taught me
Cooking on the Acoli stove
And when I visited
My mother's brother
I cooked meals
On the Lango stove.

★

In my mother's house
There are no plates:
We use the half-gourd
And the earthen dishes.
The white man's plates
Look beautiful
But you put millet bread in it
And cover it up

For a few minutes –
The plate is sweating
And soon the bottom
Of the bread is wet
And the whole loaf cold.

A loaf in a half-gourd
Returns its heat
And does not become wet
In the bottom;
And the earthen dish
Keeps the gravy hot
And the meat steaming;
And when your husband
Has returned from a hunt
Or from a long day's journey
Give him hot porridge
In a half-gourd.

And when I have
Been in the garden a whole day
Weeding or harvesting in the
    hot sun,
On my return home
Give me water
In a large half-gourd
Water from the glass
Is no use.
It reaches nowhere.

★

In my mother's house
We eat sitting on the earth
And not on trees
Like monkeys;
The young men
Sit cross legged
And a girl sits carefully

61

On one leg.
Father alone sits on the stool.
We all sit on skins
Or papyrus mats
On the earth.
The knives in my mother's house
Are for harvesting
Or for cutting up the meat
Before it is cooked:
But not for cutting millet bread.

We wash our hands clean
And attack the loaf
From all sides.
You mould a spoon
And dip it in the gravy
And eat it up.

And you use your right hand
Even if you are left-handed:
This is good manners.
Only rude fellows
Use their left hands
For breaking millet bread.

I do not know
How to cook
Like white women;
I do not enjoy
White men's foods;
And how they eat –
How could I know?
And why should I know it?

White men's stoves
Are for cooking
White men's foods.
They are not suitable
For cooking

Acoli foods
And I am afraid of them.

Ocol says
Black people's foods
  are primitive,
But what is backward about
  them?
He says
Black people's foods are dirty;
He means,
Some clumsy and dirty black
  women
Prepare food clumsily
And put them
In dirty containers.

He insists
I must eat raw eggs
Smelly, slimy yellow stuff.
He says
It is good for me!
He says
There is something in eggs
Which is good for the bones

But my bones are strong,
I can dance all night long
Listen to the song
They sang about me:

  The beautiful one
  Dances all night long
  Alyeker prevents me sleeping.
  I wait on the pathway
  She refuses to come to me
  The beautiful one
  Dances all night long.

What is the good thing in eggs?

Can it not be found
In other foods?
My husband,
I do not complain
That you eat
White men's foods.

If you enjoy them
Go ahead!
Shall we just agree
To have freedom
To eat what one likes?

7

There is No Fixed Time for Breast Feeding

My husband is angry
Because, he says,
I cannot keep time
And I do not know
How to count the years;

He asks me
How many days
There are in a year,
And how many weeks
In four moons;
But I cannot answer:
The number of moons
In nine weeks
I cannot say!
How can I tell?

Ocol has brought home
A large clock
It goes tock-tock-tock-tock
And it rings a bell.

He winds it first
And then it goes!

But I have never touched it.
I am afraid of winding it!

I wonder what causes
The noise inside it!
And what makes it go!

On the face of the clock
There are writings
And it's large single testicle
Dangles below.
It goes this way and that way
Like a sausage-fruit
In a windy storm.

I do not know
How to tell the time
Because I cannot read
The figures.
To me the clock
Is a great source of pride
It is beautiful to see
And when visitors come
They are highly impressed!

63

And Ocol has strange ways
Of saying what the time is.
In the morning
When the sun is sweet to bask in
He says
'It is Eight o'clock!'
When the cock crows
For the first time
He says
'It is Five!'
Towards the middle of the
    night,
When wizards are getting
    ready,
Ocol says
'It is Eleven!'
And after sunset
'It is Seven'.

My head gets puzzled,
Things look upside-down
As if I have been
Turning round and round
And I am dizzy.

★

If my husband insists
What exact time
He should have morning tea
And breakfast,
When exactly to have coffee
And the exact time
For taking the family
    photograph—
Lunch-time, tea time,
And supper time—
I must first look at the sun,
The cock must crow
To remind me.

In our village
When someone is going
On a long journey,
When there is a hunt
Or communal hoeing
People wake up early,
When the horizon in the East
Is aflame
And in the West
The Buffalo Star is ripe
Like a yellow and sweet mango
About to fall to the earth.

No one moves at midnight
Except wizards covered in ashes
Dancing stark naked
Armed with disembowelled frogs
And dead lizards:

Or young thieves
Looking for other men's
    daughters,
They travel fearless
Through the fiends
That sow small-pox
In the countryside;

They split the darkness
With their bare chests
They smell out their loves
Through the thick dew!

When the sun has grown up
And the poisoned tips
Of its arrows painfully bite
The backs of the men hoeing
And of the women weeding or
    harvesting.
This is when

When the sun has grown up
And the poisoned tips
Of its arrows painfully bite
The backs of the men hoeing
And of the women weeding or harvesting

You take drinking water
To the workers.

Food is taken to the fields
When the men are exhausted.
They crack the bones of chicken
And eat much peas and beans
And heaps of millet bread
As big as elephant dung.

Then they return home
Leaving behind a large field
And house-flies
Fighting over bits of food
And excreta that were thrown
    away.

When the sun
Has cooled off,
The men and youths
Visit the traps and pits,
They hunt edible rats,
Or hook fish
From the streams.

Others cut wooden dishes
Out of logs
Or make ropes for the cows
Or weave baskets
For the chicken house;
They repair the roofs
Of the granaries
Or make patterns on half-gourds.

You hear the flutes
Of the herdsmen
Bringing the cattle home.
The flute-songs mingle
With the lowing of the bulls.

A man listens
To the roar of his own bull
And shouts praises to it.
But no one praises another's
    bull,
Not even the bull of his brother.

The young boys
Who tend the goats
Take turns to make
The outdoor fire.

★

The fortunate mother
Of a good daughter
Sits outside her hut,
Her back turned to
The outdoor fire,
Her legs fully stretched
And she congratulates herself.

But if your daughter
Has no manners
If she is so loose
That men sleep with her
Even in the grass,
Then, even if you are ill
You must go to the well
To draw water
And the *nanga* players
Will sing you a song:

The mother of the beautiful girl
Dies on the way to the well
As if she has no daughter
Her girl has no manners
What is to be done?
The mother of the girl

66

Dies on the grinding stone
In the bush to collect firewood!

At the *orak* dance
A good girl
Whose mother is blind
Dances vigorously
And glances at the sun,
She returns home
Before sunset.
A good daughter
Releases her mother
She sits around the evening fire
And tells folk tales
To her younger ones.

★

My husband says
I am useless
Because I waste time,
He quarrels
Because, he says,
I am never punctual.
He says
He has no time to waste.
He tells me
Time is money.

Ocol does not chat
With me,
He never jokes
With anybody,
He says
He has no time
To sit around the evening fire.

When my husband
Is reading a new book

Or when he is
Sitting in his sofa,
His face covered up
Completely with the big
    newspaper
So that he looks
Like a corpse,
Like a lone corpse
In the tomb,

He is so silent!
His mouth begins
To decay!

If a child cries
Or has a cough
Ocol storms like a buffalo,
He throws things
At the child;
He says
He does not want
To hear noises,
That children's cries
And coughs disturb him!

Is this not the talk
Of a witch?
What music is sweeter
Than the cries of children?

A homestead in which
The cries of children
Are not heard,
Where the short little songs
Are not repeated endlessly,
Where the brief sobs
And brotherly accusations
And false denials
Are not heard!

67

A homestead where
Children's exreta is not
Scattered all over the swept
    compound
And around the granaries,

Where all the pots and earthen
    dishes
Are safe
Because there are no
Silly ones to break them.
No clumsy hands
Trying hard to please mother
And breaking half-gourds,

Who but a witch
Would like to live
In a homestead
Where all the grown-ups
Are so clean after the rains,
Because there are no
Muddy fat kids
To fall on their bosoms
After dancing in the rains
And playing in the mud?

At the lineage shrine
The prayers are for child birth!
At the *ogodo* dance
The woman who struts
And dances proudly,
That is the mother of many,
That is the fortunate one;
And she dances
And looks at her own shadow.

★

Time has become

My husband's master
It is my husband's husband.
My husband runs from place to
    place
Like a small boy,
He rushes without dignity.

And when visitors have arrived
My husband's face darkens,
He never asks you in,
And for greeting
He says
'What can I do for you?'

★

I do not know
How to keep the white man's
    time.
My mother taught me
The way of the Acoli
And nobody should
Shout at me
Because I know
The customs of our people!
When the baby cries
Let him suck milk
From the breast.
There is no fixed time
For breast feeding.

When the baby cries
It may be he is ill;
The first medicine for a child
Is the breast.
Give him milk
And he will stop crying,
And if he is ill
Let him suck the breast

While the medicine-man
Is being called
From the beer party.

Children in our homestead
Do not sleep at fixed times:
When sleep comes
Into their head
They sleep,
When sleep leaves their head
They wake up.

When a child is dirty
Give him a wash,
You do not first look at the sun!
When there is no water
In the house
You cannot wash the child
Even if it is time
For his bath!
Listen
My husband,
In the wisdom of the Acoli
Time is not stupidly split up
Into seconds and minutes,
It does not flow
Like beer in a pot
That is sucked
Until it is finished.

It does not resemble
A loaf of millet bread
Surrounded by hungry youths
From a hunt;
It does not get finished
Like vegetables in the dish.

A lazy youth is rebuked,
A lazy girl is slapped,

A lazy wife is beaten,
A lazy man is laughed at
Not because they waste time
But because they only destroy
And do not produce.

And when famine
Invades your villages
And women take their baskets
To go and beg food
In the next village
Strangers will sleep with them!
They will have your wives
And what can you say?

★

Ocol laughs at me
Because, he says,
I do not know
The names of the moons,
That I do not know
How many moons in a year
And the number of Sabbaths
In one moon.

The Sabbath is a day
For Christians
When Protestants and Catholics
    shout
And suffer from headaches.

The Acoli did not
Set aside a special day
For *Jok*;
When misfortune hits the
    homestead
The clansmen gather
And offer sacrifices
To the ancestors:

69

When the rains
Refuse to come
The Rain-Cock* prepares a feast.
A goat is speared
In the wilderness
And the elders offer prayers
To *Jok.*

★

We all know the moon—
It elopes,
Climbs the hill
And falls down;

It lights up the night,
Youths like it,
Wizards hate it,
And hyenas howl
When the moon
Shines into their eyes.

Periodically each woman
Sees the moon,
And when a young girl
Has seen it
For the first time
It is a sign
That the garden is ready
For sowing,
And when the gardener comes
Carrying two bags of live seeds
And a good strong hoe
The rich red soil
Swells with a new life.

Turning your back

To your husband
Is a serious taboo,
But when the baby
Is still toothless froth,
When you see the moon
You turn your back
To your husband.

If you do not resist
The great appetite
Then your child becomes
Sickly and thin
His knees become
Soft like porridge,
He will become pregnant
And the weight of his diseased
    stomach
Will prevent him
From standing up.

I do not know
The names of the moons
Because the Acoli
Do not name their moons.

During the *Ager* period
Millet is sown,
Just before the rains
And as they sow
They raise much dust.

When the rains return
We say
The rains have fallen
The period is called
Poto-kot
Then the millet seeds germinate.

* The priest of rain, who presides during the ceremony for rain.

Sometimes the rains come early
Sometimes they return late.
When the millet
Begins to flower
And the time
For the harvest is approaching
All the granaries are empty:

And hunger begins
To bite peoples' tummies,
This period
Is called *Odunge*,
Because fierce hunger burns
People's insides
And they drink
Vegetable soups
To deaden the teeth
Of the fire.

And as the millet
Begins to get ready for the
    harvest,
Some women ask,
Is this not my own garden?
They take their harvest knives
And a small basket,
They cut one head here
And another one there,
And when someone laughs,
They ask,
Whose garden have I spoiled?
So the period
Just before the harvest
Is called
Abalo-pa-nga?

The Acoli know
The Wet Season
And the Dry Season.

Wet Season means
Hard work in the fields,
Sowing, weeding, harvesting.
It means waking up before
    dawn,
It means mud
And thick dew.
Herdboys dislike it.
Lazy people hate it.

Dry Season means pleasures,
It means dancing,
It means hunting
In freshly burnt plains.

You hear *otole* dance drums
And funeral songs,
You hear the horns and trumpets
And the moonlight dance songs
Floating in the air.

Youths in small groups
Go on the *apet* hunting
    expeditions.
Great hunters stay alone
In the wilderness
Smoking the carcass of the cob
Or the buffalo.

Others go off to Pajule
To look for bridewealth,
For if you have no sister
Then kill an elephant.
You sell the teeth
And marry a wife,
Then you call your son
Ocan, because you are poor!

Dry Season means wooing

71

And eloping with girls,
It means the *moko* dance
When youths and girls
Get stuck to one another!

★

My husband says,
My head is numb and empty
Because, he says,
I cannot tell
When our children were born.

I know that Okang
My first born
Was born at the beginning
Of the Dry Season
And my little girl
In the middle of the rains.
Okang was born
In the middle of the famine
Called *Abongo-wang-dako*.
They say
One night a man
Was so hungry
He got up
And felt his wife's eyes
To see if she was asleep
So that he might
Inspect the cooking pots.

And Atoo was born
After the smallpox fiends
Had just left the homestead.
The fiends found
Many people with bad hearts
There was much quarrelling
And jealousy among women
And so many people perished.

I lost my father too,
That is why
The little girl was called Atoo.

★

A person's age
Is seen by looking at him or her.
A girl is grown up
When her breasts have come;
A young man's voice breaks
And hair appears
On his face
And below his belly button.

When a girl sees the moon
She is ripe,
After bearing three children
She begins to wither
And soon she becomes
A mother-in-law.
Then she is deeply respected.

A person's age
Is shown by what he or she does
It depends on what he or she is,
And on what kind of person
He or she is.

You may be a giant
Of a man,
You may begin
To grow grey hair
You may be bold
And toothless with age,
But if you are unmarried
You are nothing.

★

Ocol tells me
Things I cannot understand,
He talks
About a certain man,
Jesus.
He says
The man was born
Long ago
In the country of white men.

He says
When Jesus was born
White men began
To count years:
From one, then it became ten.
Then one hundred
Then one thousand
And now it is

One thousand
Nine hundred
And sixty six.

My husband says
Before this man was born
White men counted years
    backwards.
Starting with the biggest number
Then it became
One thousand
Then one hundred
Then ten,
And when it became one
Then Jesus was born.

I cannot understand all this
I do not understand it at all!

8

I Am Ignorant of the Good Word in the Clean Book

My husband
Looks down upon me;
He says
I am a mere pagan,
I do not know
The way of God.
He says
I am ignorant
Of the good word
In the Clean Book
And I do not have

A Christian name.
Ocol dislikes me
Because, he says,
Jok is in my head
And I like visiting
The diviner-priest
Like my mother!

He says
He is ashamed of me
Because when the *Jok*

73

Song of Lawino

In my head
Has been provoked
It throws me down
As if I have fits.

Ocol laughs at me
Because I cannot
Cross myself properly

_In the name of the Father
And of the Son
And the Clean Ghost_

And I do not understand
The confession,
And I fear
The bushy-faced, fat-bellied
    padré
Before whom people kneel
When they pray.

★

I refused to join
The Protestant catechist class,
Because I did not want
To become a house-girl,
I did not want
To become a slave
To a woman with whom
I may share a man.

Oh how young girls
Labour to buy a name!
You break your back
Drawing water
For the wives
Of the teachers,
The skin of your hand

Hardens and peels off
Grinding millet and simsim.
You hoe their fields,
Split firewood,
You cut grass for thatching
And for starting fires,
You smear their floors
With cow dung and black soil
And harvest their crops.

And when they are eating
They send you to play games
To play the board game
Under the mango tree!

And girls gather
Wild sweet potatoes
And eat them raw
As if there is a famine,
And they are so thin
They look like
Cattle that have dysentery!

You work as if
You are a newly eloped girl!
The wives of protestant
Church teachers and priests
Are a happy lot.
They sit with their legs
    stretched out
And bask in the morning sun.
All they know
Is hatching a lot of children.

★

My elder sister
Was christened Erina,
She was a Protestant

74

But she suffered bitterly
In order to buy the name
And her loin beads
No longer fitted her!

One Sunday
I followed her
Into the Protestant church:
A big man stood
Before the people.
His hand was lifted up,
My sister said
He was blessing the people.
The man had no rosary,
He wore a long black gown
And a wide white robe
He held a little shiny saucer:
It had small pieces of something.
The name of the man
Was Eliya
And he was calling people
To come and eat
Human flesh!
He put little bits
In their hands
And they ate it up!

Then he took a cup,
He said
There was human blood
In the cup
And he gave it
To the people
To drink!

I ran out of the Church,
I was very sick!

O! Protestants eat people!
They are all wizards,
They exhume corpses
For dinner!

★

I once joined
The Catholic Evening Speakers'
    Class
But I did not stay long
I ran away,
I ran away from shouting
Meaninglessly in the evenings
Like parrots
Like the crow birds

Maria the Clean Woman
Mother of the Hunchback*
Pray for us
Who spoil things
Full of graciya.

The things they shout
I do not understand,
They shout anyhow
They shout like mad people.
The padré shouts words,
You cannot understand,
And he does not seem
To care in the least
Whether his hearers
Understand him or not;
A strange language they speak
These Christian diviner-priests,
And the white nuns
Think the girls understand

* See footnote on p. 94

75

What they are saying
And are annoyed
When the girls laugh.
One night
The moon was very bright
And in the distance
The 'get-stuck' dance drums
Were throbbing vigorously,

The teacher was very drunk
His eyes were like rotting
    tomatoes.
We guessed he was teaching
Something about the Clean
    Ghost.

He shouted words at us
And we shouted back at him,
Agitated and angry
Like the *okwik* birds
Chasing away the kite
From their nest.

He shouted angrily
As if he uttered abuses,
We repeated the same words
Shouting back at him
As when you shout
Insults at somebody's mother!

We repeated the meaningless
    phrases
Like the yellow birds
In the *lajanawara* grass.

The teacher was an Acoli
But he spoke the same language
As the white priests.
His nose was blocked

And he tried
To force his words
Through his blocked nose.

He sounded like
A loosely strung drum.

The teacher's name
Was Bicenycio Lagucu.
He was very drunk
And he smiled, bemused.

The drums of the 'get-stuck'
    dance
Thundered in the distance
And the songs came floating
In the air.

The milk
In our ripe breasts boiled,
And little drops of sweat
Appeared on our foreheads,
You think of the pleasures
Of the girls
Dancing before their lovers,

Then you look at the teacher
Barking meaninglessly
Like the yellow monkey.

In the arena
They began to sing my song,
We could hear it faintly
Passing through the air
Like the thin smoke
From an old man's pipe:
    O! Lawino!
    Come let me see you
    Daughter of Lenga-moi

You think of the pleasures
Of the girls
Dancing before their lovers,
Then you look at the teacher
Barking meaninglessly
Like the yellow monkey.

Who has just shot up
Young woman come home!
O Lawino!
Chief of the girls
My love come
That I may elope with you
Daughter of the Bull
Come that I may touch you.

The teacher drummed
His meaningless phrases
Through his blocked nose;
He was getting more drunk.
Thick white froth
Formed around his mouth
As if he had just fallen down
With fits.

Pray for us
Who spoil things
Full of graciya

And when he shouted
The word 'graciya'
(Whatever the word meant)
Saliva squirted from his mouth
And froth flew
Like white ants from his mouth,
The smelly drops
Landed on our faces
Like heavily loaded houseflies
Fresh from a fresh excreta heap!

And when he belched
The smell of the rotting beer
Hit you like a brick,
And when he belched
His mouth filled with hot beer
From his belly

And he noisily swallowed this
back.

The collar of the teacher's white
shirt
Was black with dirt,
He was sweating profusely
And his cheeks were rough
Like the tongue of the ox.

The comb never touched his
head,
His hair resembled the elephant
grass,
Tall and wiry
The teacher looked like a witch.

And he endlessly
Drummed his meaningless
words
Through his blocked nose,
And we shouted the words back
at him,
And the moonlight dance drums
Thundered in the distance.
And the songs came floating
From beyond his hills.
My comrades
Are dancing in the moonlight
And I
Sitting before the ugly man,
Before the man
With the rough skin,
The man
Whose body smells!

The girls are dancing
Before their lovers,
Shaking their waists

To the rhythm of the drums;
And I
Sitting like stale bread
On the rubbish heap;

My companions are gay
They are dancing
And singing meaningful songs,
In the arena
They are singing
My song;

And the boys
Are whispering sweet words
Into the girls' ears
And our teacher
Is drunk!

Anger welled up inside me
Burning my chest like bile,
I stood up
And two other girls stood up,
We walked out,
Out of that cold hall
With the stone floor.
We ran fast,
Away from the ugly man
Away from the meaningless
    shouts
Like parrots,
Like the yellow birds
In the *lajanawara* grass.

We crossed the stream
And climbed the gentle rise
Straight into the arena.
We joined the line of friends
And danced among our age-
    mates

And sang songs we understood,
Relevant and meaningful songs,
Songs about ourselves:

> *O father*
> *Gather the bridewealth*
> *That I may bring a woman*
>   *home,*
> *O the woman of my bosom*
> *The beautiful one*
> *Prevents me from sleeping.*
> *The woman of my bosom.*

> *If anyone troubles my beloved*
> *I shall shed tears of blood;*
> *The woman of my bosom*
> *Prevents me from sleeping.*
> *O father,*
> *If I die,*
> *I will become a vengeance ghost,*
> *The woman of my bosom*
> *Prevents me from sleeping.*

We danced with vigour
And sweat poured
Down our backs,
Youthful sweat
From healthy bodies.

★

Let the fool
Continue to deceive himself!
Who has ever prevented
The cattle from the salt lick?

The time when youth should
    meet youth
Is wasted in shouting things

79

No one understands,
Is spent in singing
Meaningless songs
That no one believes in.

The milk in your breast
Boils painfully.
Your breasts must be touched,
Rubbed on the cool chest of
    your beloved
So that the pricking pains
May be relieved.
The heads of the young men
Reject the pillows
And prefer
The arms of their lovers.

But they lock you up
Inside a cold hall
As if you are sheep,
And they lock up
All the girls
In one cold hall,
And the boys
In another cold hall.

And the young men
Sleep alone
Cold, like knives
Without handles.

And the spears
Of the lone hunters,
The trusted right-hand spears
Of young bulls
Rust in the dewy cold
Of the night.

★

But look!
Who comes with
The large headed club?

The teacher, still drunk.
He too is coming
To hunt for girls
At the 'get-stuck' dance!
He joined the line of youths
But they pushed him away!
He danced at the edge
Singing properly,
His large owl-head
Moving this way
And that way
To the rhythm of the drums.

Shameless
The ugly man
Whispered something in my ear!
And touched my breast
With the rough palm
Of his bony hand
Cutting it as if with
An old rusty knife.

I spat in his face.

He said
He would dismiss me
From the Evening Speakers'
    Class,
And if I am so stupid,
I will never get
Anything from the purse
In his trouser pocket.

Don't touch me
You rough-skinned aged thing!

Who cares for your stupid
   shoutings
In the evening?
Let go my hand
Syphilis man!
Who can you buy
To spread your death!

★

And all the teachers
Are alike,
They have sharp eyes
For girls' full breasts;
Even the padrés
Who are not allowed
To marry
Are troubled by health,
Even the fat-stomached
Who cannot see
His belly button
Feels better
When he touches
A girl's breasts,
And those who listen
To the confessions
Peep through the port-hole
And stab the breasts
With their glances.

★

My husband rejects me
Because, he says
I have no Christian name.

He says
Lawino is not enough.
He says
Acoli names are *Jok* names
And they do not sound good.
They are primitive, he insists,
And he is a progressive man

Ocol wanted me
To be baptized 'Benedeta',
He has christened
One daughter 'Marta'.
The other took
The name of the mother of the
   Hunchback!

   Maria the Clean Woman
   Mother of the Hunchback

His first born son is Jekcon
And the second he calls Paraciko.
One of his illegitimate sons is
   Tomcon
And the other Gulyelmo Iriko.*

My husband rejects Acoli
   names,
Meaningful names,
Names that I can pronounce.
He says

They are *Jok* names
And he was nothing
To do with *Jok*.

* *Jekcon*: Jackson
  Paraciko: Francis
  Tomcon: Thompson
  Gulyelmo: William
  Iriko: Erik

Song of Lawino

He says
He has left behind
All sinful things
And all superstitions and fears.
He says
He has no wish
To be associated any more
With the devil.

Pagan names, he says,
Belong to sinners
Who will burn
In everlasting fires:
Ocol insists
He must be called
By his Christian name!

But my husband's name
Is so difficult to pronounce;
It sounds something like
Medikijedeki Gilirigoloyo.*

It sounds to me like
'Give the people more
   vegetables,
Foxes make holes in the pathway',

It sound like a praise name
Uttered by a stammerer!
What is the meaning of 'Marta'?
Gulyelmo, Iriko, Jekcon,
Are these names of ancestors?

★

My Bull name is Eliya Alyeker,

I ate the name
Of the Chief of Payira,
Eliya Aliker,
Son of Awic.

Bull names are given
To Chiefs of girls
Because like bulls
They lead their age-mates,
Like the full moon at night
They dominate the stars.

They are names
Of great chiefs
And great men of war.

Is 'Benedeta' a Bull name?
Is 'Maria' a Bull name
In the white man's country?

Apiyo and Acen
Are *Jok* names
Twins are Joks,
And are deeply respected.
Akelo is the one
Who comes after twins,
Ajok and Ajara
Grow extra fingers or toes,
Adoc comes out
Of the belly feet first.

All these are *Jok*
And they are feared and
   respected.
When a girl is called Adong
Her father died
Just before she was born.

* *Medikijedeki*: Milchizedek
  Gilirigoloyo: Gregory

82

Song of Lawino

Akot does not mean
'Born in the rains',
But 'afterbirth
Contained bubbles of water',
And this is a sign of rain.
The daughter of
A woman with a black heart
Who kills people with poisons
Is called Akwir or Anek.

Some names are names of
    sorrows.
Alobo, Abur, Ayiko, Woko
That Fate has thrown
A large basket
To be filled
With dead children

> Fate has brought troubles
> Son of my mother
> Fate has thrown me a basket,
> It all began as a joke
> Suffering is painful
> It began before I was born.

★

My father's name
Is Otoo Lenga-moi,
He ate the title Lenga-moi
In the battle in the Hills.
Ocol's grandfather's title
Is Lutany-moi
You earn the moi
With your spear
Or gun or sword.

Is 'Tomcon' a *Jok* name?
'Paraciko', is it a battle honour?
'Bicenycio' and 'Iriko'

Are these praise names
That white men shout
When they dance their 'get-
    stuck' dance?
Or are they mourning names?

The first born
May have a name
But he is always called Okang,
He is the first
To listen to the songs
Of the birds;
He is proof
That the woman is not barren;
He is the owner of the shrine
That shall be built
In honour of his father,
He is respected.

The one who follows Okang
Is called Oboi.
He is always jealous,
He fights with his brother
And fights for his brother.
The third son is called Odai
And the last son is Cogo.
If you hit his head
With your finger
His mother will throw
Things at you;
Because that is the child
Of which a mother is most fond.

★

Who understands
The meaning of the Christian
    names?
The names they read for

83

The names of white men
That they give to children
When they put water on their
    heads,
What do they mean?

To me
They all sound
Like empty tins,
Old rusty tins
Thrown down
From the roof-top.

9

From the
Mouth of Which River?

When I was in the Evening
    Speakers' Class
We recited the Faith of the
    Messengers
And Our Father who is in
    Skyland,
We sang Greetings to Maria
We learnt:

> *Glory shine on the body of the*
>   *Father*
> *And on the body of the Son*
> *And on the body of the Clean*
>   *Ghost*

We recited the Prayer for saying
    Yes
And the Prayer for Love,
The Prayer for Trust,
The Greetings of the beautiful
    men
With birds' wings,
And the Dekalogu,

The Ten Instructions of the
    Hunchback.

But our teachers
Hated questions.
Protestant and Catholic priests
Are all the same—
They do not like questions.

When they mount the rostrum
To preach
They shout and shout
And most of what they say
I do not follow.
But as soon as they stop shouting
They run away fast,
They never stop a little while
To answer even one question,

Immediately
They start collecting
The gifts.
You hear:

Who sows a little
Will reap a little
Who sows much
Will reap much
It is not by force
The Hunchback thanks those
    who give with soft hearts

Do they buy the places
In Skyland with money?
The stools
On the right hand of the
    Hunchback,
Are these reserved
For moneyed fellows,

Fat-bellied men
The backs of whose necks
Resemble the buttocks of the
    hippo,
And green oils
Ooze out of the lined necks?

Those who will
Surround the Hunchback,
Will they be
The three-chinned ones
Who are not used to the heat
And should not go
To the place below
Because it does not befit them
And it is too warm for them?

★

The teachers
Of the Evening Speakers' Class
Hate questions.
If you go to the Padré
You provoke a fight.

You take the road
And go to the Nun,
The young woman
Is fierce like
A wounded buffalo girl,
She screams
As if someone has
Stabbed her at the death spot.
And the black teachers
Are angry
They say
Asking too many questions
Befits only Martin Luther
And the stupid stubborn
    Protestants.
They say,
Asking a lot of silly questions
Cannot be tolerated,
And the Padré quarrels
And his goatee beard
Shakes furiously.

★

We sang the Faith of the
    Messengers
Like parrots,
I did not understand it at all!
I thought about it
In my own head
But I could get nowhere,
And there was nobody
To turn to.
The Padré and the Nun are the
    same,
They only quarrel
They are angry with me
As if it was I
Who prevented them marrying.

To them
The good children
Are those
Who ask no questions,
Who accept everything
Like the tomb
Which does not reject
Even a dead leper!
Who accept everything
Like the rubbish pit,
Like the pit-latrine
Which does not reject
Even dysentery.

And those good children
Who ask no questions
Are liked,
They are given oranges
And guavas and bananas
They take a ride
In the Padré's car.
The Nun pats them on their backs
And says my son you are good!

★

We recited
The Faith of the Messengers
Like the yellow birds
In the *lajanawara* grass

The teacher shouted
As if half-mad
And we shouted back:

> *I accept the Hunchback*
> *The Padre who is very strong*
> *Moulder of Skyland and*
> *Earth ...*

My mother
Was a well-known potter,
She moulded large pots,
Vegetable pots,
And beautiful long necked jars.
She made water pots
And smoking pipes
And vegetable dishes.
And large earthen vessels for
    bath.
She dug the clay
From the mouth of the Oyitino
    River.
The place
Was well-known among potters.

I heard about it
When I was a small girl,
And when my breasts emerged
I went with my mother
And helped her carrying the
    clay.

The Hunchback
Where did he dig the clay
For moulding things?
Where is the pot
He dug the clay
For moulding Skyland,
And the clay for moulding Earth?
From the mouth of which River?
When my mother
Has brought the clay
From the River
She leaves it to season overnight.
The next day
She beats it with the wooden
    hammer
And then she moulds

The pots and dishes
And none of her works
Crack when fired!

When Skyland was not yet there
And Earth was not yet moulded
Nor the Stars
Nor the Moon,
When there was nothing,
Where did the Hunchback live?

Where did the Hunchback
Dig the clay for moulding things,
The clay for moulding Skyland
The clay for moulding Earth
The clay for moulding Moon
The clay for moulding the Stars?
Where is the spot
Where it was dug,
On the mouth of which River?

And when the Hunchback
Was digging the clay
Where did he stand?
And when he brought home
The clay for moulding things
Where did he put the clay
To season overnight?
And when he was beating it
With the wooden hammer
On which rock
Did the Hunchback put the clay?

★

My husband
Has read at Makerere University.
He has read deeply and widely,
But if you ask him a question
He says

You are insulting him;
He opens up with a quarrel
He begins to look down upon you
Saying
You ask questions
That are a waste of time!

He says
My questions are silly questions,
Typical questions from village
  girls.
Questions of uneducated people,
Useless questions from
  untutored minds.

My husband says
I have a tiny little brain
And it is not trained,
I cannot see things intelligently,
I cannot see things sharply.
He says
Even if he is tried
To answer my questions
I would not understand
What he was saying
Because the language he speaks
Is different from mine
So that even if he
Spoke to me in Acoli
I would still need an interpreter.

My husband says
Some of the answers
Cannot be given in Acoli
Which is a primitive language
And is not rich enough
To express his deep wisdom.
He says the Acoli language
Has very few words

It is not like the white man's
    language
Which is rich and very beautiful
A language fitted for discussing
    deep thoughts.

Ocol says
He has no time to waste
Discussing things with a thing
    like me
Who has not been to school.
He says
A university man
Can only have useful talk
With another university man or
    woman.
And that it is funny,
That he should stoop so low
Even to listen
To my questions.

And when he says
These things to me
He does not look me in the face,
He turns his back
And talks casually
While doing some other work.

And when the Padré
Hears these questions
He threatens you with his beard!
When a Nun
Hears the questions
She says,
You should repeat
The Prayers for Faith.

★

I think about these questions
In my head
And my head begins to ache,
And my neck begins to pain,
But who can I ask?
Where can I go?

I am not a shy woman
I am not afraid of anybody
And I am not easily browbeaten.
I know that the person who asks
Has done no wrong,
I will not be frightened
By those who say
Asking questions is mortal sin
That will take a person
To the Place Below.

But I swallow the questions,
They burn inside me
Like a bee
That has gone into the ear;
And my eyes redden
With frustration
And I tremble
With anger.

★

When the Hunchback was not
    yet there
Before he had moulded himself
What things were there?

When Skyland was not yet
    moulded
And there was no Earth,
No Stars
No Moon

When Chief Hunchback was not
    yet there
Before he had moulded himself,

Where did he get the clay
For moulding things?
The clay for moulding himself
Where did he get it,
From the mouth of which River?
When the Hunchback was not
    yet there
And his head was not yet
    moulded
And his eyes
And his hands
And his legs
When his heart was not yet
    there,
How did he find
The clay for moulding things
Before he had any eyes?
The clay for moulding the
    Hunchback
Where was it dug from?
From the mouth of which River?

How did the Hunchback
Dig the clay for moulding things
Before his hands were moulded?
The wooden digging stick
For digging the clay,
The wooden hammer
For beating the clay
For moulding himself,
How did he hold the wooden
    hammer
And the digging stick?
Whose hands did he borrow?

And when he was digging

The clay for moulding himself
Whose legs did he use
For standing up?

Where did Chief Hunchback
Get his head
For thinking about moulding
    himself,
For beginning to think
About moulding himself
And what shape and size
He should be?

Where did the Hunchback
Find the hands,
The hands for moulding himself
Where did he find them?
How did he mould his hands
Before he had any hands?

★

On the way to the well
To draw water
In the bush
Collecting dry firewood
I think about these questions
When I am grinding millet
Or on the rocks
Drying the cassava mash,
On the way to the garden
Early in the morning
Through the thick dew,
In the night
I cannot sleep
But my head just stops
Like a broken down car!

★

And the questions
Are numerous like grass,
If you begin to ask them
They flow endlessly
Like the Nile waters,
They burn endlessly
Like the red fire
At the altar!
You wish there was
No other work
So that you may sit
For as long as you like;

And you wish
You were lucky
To find someone to help you;
Someone who has genuinely
Read deeply and widely
And not someone like my
   husband
Whose preoccupation
Is to boast in the market place
Showing off to people!

You wish you were lucky
To find someone to assist you
Who does not shout
Like house-flies
When disturbed
From an excreta heap!
Who does not shout meaninglessly
Like the Padre;
Who listens,
And does not get annoyed
So easily like the Nun:
Who does not boast
Like the teachers of the Evening
   Speakers' Class.

You consider the birth of Christ:
They say
His mother did not know a man.
They also say,
The bridewealth had already
   been paid,

Among our People
When a girl has
Accepted a man's proposal
She gives a token,
And then she visits him
In his bachelor's hut
To try his manhood.

Before the bridewealth is paid
The man puts his cheeks
On the girl's bosom
And if the girl is lucky
She gets a stomach!

And when they teach
That the Mother of Christ
Did not know a man
I cannot understand it.

But the teachers of religion
Hate questions;
A young tree that is bending
They do not like to straighten.
Whether they do it purposely,
Whether they themselves
Have no answers
I do not know,
But I know
They hate questions.

★

10

*The Last Safari to Pagak**

My husband quarrels bitterly.
He says
I do not know hygiene
And I do not know
How to look after the sick.
He says
I do not know
The use of quinine,
And I have not been taught
How to prevent diseases.
My man is ashamed of me
Because my father
Was a well-known diviner-priest;
He says
He is sick of my superstitions
and fears.

And he fears
What the neighbours say
Because my mother brought
Some powerful anti-poison
medicine,
To counter the deadly poisons
Of the childless woman
In our homestead.
Some had brought *agugu*
Others brought *adraka*

With which to kill all the
children.

My husband complains
That I encourage visitors
Who should not
Come into his house,
Because they bring dirt and
house-flies!

He says
My old relatives smell horribly.
And they have terrible diseases,
Leprosy and tuberculosis
And their bodies itch.
He says
These diseases will be
Transmitted to the children.
He has warned me
That my father's sister
Has lice in her hair
And jiggers in her feet.
She should not visit me!

My husband says these things
In broad daylight.
He speaks aloud,

* Pagak is the place of no return, Death's homestead.

91

He does not care
Whether my relatives
Hear him or not.
And when a storm is threatening,
He says
There are no beds
In his house
For villagers!

My husband says
Villagers soil his chairs
And bed sheets,
He says
They ruin his nicely polished
    floor
With the mud in their feet.

He cares little
About his relatives either.
Of his own mother,
Ocol says
She smokes some nauseating
    tobacco
And spits all over the place
And she keeps bed bugs
In her loin cloth.
And when his mother
Comes to visit him,
Ocol locks the doors
And says
He has an important meeting
In the town!

My husband complains
About food.
You would think
He earns sand!
He told his mother's brother
There was no food

Because he had not written
A letter!

The son of the Bull
Does not allow the children
To visit my mother,
He says
He does not like
The feeding of grandmothers
Because the children
Eat all the time.

Ocol says
The way his mother
Brings up children
Only leads
To ignorance, poverty and
    disease.
He swears
He has no confidence
In the wisdom of the Acoli.

★

My husband despises me
Because I fear
The kite with the flame
In its anus.

He says
No such things exist.
It is my eyes
That are sick
And only foolish superstitions
Make me see these things.
But my husband believes
Some people see
The beautiful men
With the wings of vultures

Flying through the air!

My husband has threatened
To beat me
If I visit the diviner-priest again.
He says
The hair-poison does not exist,
That it is hook-worm
That troubles the people.

Ocol condemns diviner-priests
And Acoli herbalists.
He says
They are all liars
Who deceive fools,
And robs people's chickens,
Goats, sheep, cattle and money.

Their so-called medicines
Are dirty mixtures
Of all sorts of things
Collected from the bush
And mixed in beer.

He says
The medicine gourds are filthy,
And the herbs
Are drunk from unhygienic cups.

My husband agrees
That sometimes by accident
Some of the herbs are effective.
He also admits
That not all who
Enter the white man's hospital
Walk home on their own feet,
But are carried away
In comfortable beds
Painless, free of troubles,

No more bothered by hunger or
    anger
Or the complaints of wives!

When the fiends
That brings smallpox
Visit the homestead,
Ocol does not go
To the shrine of the ancestors.
He says
It is foolish to do so,
We should have our arms
    scratched
And some corrosive poisons
Put in the wounds.

He says
When we suffer misfortune
We should say:

> *Look Mariya*
> *Mother of the Hunchback ...*

We should pray to Joseph
And Petero, and Luka
And the other ancestors of
    white men!
He says
It is stupid superstition
To pray to our ancestors
To avert the smallpox,
But we should pray
To the messengers of the
    Hunchback
To intercede for us.

My husband wears
A small crucifix
On his neck,

93

And all his daughters
Wear rosaries.

But he prohibits me
From wearing the elephant tail
    necklace,
He once beat me
For wearing the toe of the
    edible rat
And the horn of the rhinoceros
And the jaw-bone of the
    alligator.

A large snake
Once fell down from the roof
Of the cold hall!
The Nun who was teaching
The Evening Speakers' Class
Grabbed her large crucifix
And pressed it on her bosom,
Closed her eyes
And said something
We could not understand.

My husband says
The cowry shells,
The colobus-monkey hair,
The dog's horn charms
Are all useless things.

He says
Only foolish backward folk
Uneducated simple fellows
Who live in the shadow of fear
Carry these dirty things!

When a bull disease
Has knocked me down
Or when the ghost in my head
Is provoked
And threatens to cause ill-health,

When a child
Has been cursed by his uncle
Or when the Evil Eye
Has attacked my daughter,

My husband does not allow me
To visit the diviner-priest,
The goat cannot be sacrificed,
And no *Jok* dances
Can be danced.

And when it is *Jok* Omara
That has caused madness,
Or Odude or Ayweya
That has brought troubles,
When *Jok* Rubanga*
Has broken someone's back
Or *Jok* Odude
Has tied up a woman's womb,
And the husband
Cries over his lost bridewealth,
Saying,
What is marriage without
    childbirth?

Ocol laughs,
Ocol says,
The ways of fools are dark
And they are foolish beyond
    compare!

★

* The name of the Christian God in Lwo is *Rubanga*. This is also the name of the ghost that causes tuberculosis of the spine, hence Hunchback.

My husband
Once smashed up the rattle
   gourd,
Cut open the drum,
And chased away the diviner-
   priest
From his late father's homestead.
The old man walked away,
His headgear waving
His ankle bells jangling
   rhythmically
And the large monkey-skin bag
Dangling on his neck.

People whistled in amazement,
They asked,
What ghost has captured
The head of Ocol?

My husband took an axe
And threatened to cut the
   Okango
That grew on his father's
   shrine.
His mother fell down under the
   tree,
She said
Cut me first
Then cut the sacred tree!

He threw down the axe
And went to the church.
He knelt before
The stone picture of Joseph
And mumbled things
I could not understand.

★

I do not know
The white man's names of
   diseases,
I do not know
The names of their medicines,
I cannot measure
The heat of the body
With the white man's glass rod
Because my hand trembles
And I cannot read it.

When my child is unwell
I see it from his watering nose,
The hair of his body stands up
And his lips are parched,
I see that he is not bright,
I do not read the names of
   diseases from books.

I hear him cry
And his eyes water,
I hear the noise from his
   stomach
The worms complaining;

He is pale
As if he has been playing in
   ashes,
You hear his chest crackling,
He has no appetite,
And he is aggressive but tired
   and weak;
He is troublesome,
He wants this thing and that
   thing,
Then he does not want this
   thing
And does not want that thing.

His body feels hot like fire,
And he sits by the fire
In the middle of a hot afternoon.

When my child is ill
I try the various Acoli herbs,
I try the medicines
My mother showed me:

The roots of *bomo*
For stomach aches
It kills poisons
As well as worms.

The roots of *omwombye*
Is chewed for bad throats,
A drop in the eye
Kills the pains
And removes the Evil Eye's
    sting.
When the eyes are bursting with
    pain
Put some *akeyo* in a pot.
Cook it for some time,
Then expose the eyes
To the steam from the pot;
This burns up the spears
That were in the eye.

The shoots of *lapena*
For coughs and sore throats—
You put some salt in it
And chew it!
The shoots of *lapena* and *olim*
Are chewed when they have
Removed the blockage in the
    throat.

Fresh wounds are treated

With *ogali* or *pobo*,
The sticky juices
Gum up the broken skins
And the bitter poison
Keeps the house-flies at bay.

My mother showed me many
    medicines,
Medicines for leprosy and yaws,
For difficult childbirth and
    barrenness
For men whose spears
Refuse to stand up,
Lazy spears
That sleep on their bellies
Like earthworms!
Medicines for snake bites,
Medicines for breasts
That dry up too soon
Big milkless breasts
Full of fibre
Like the fruit of the *barusus*
    palm!

If my child is ill
I try the various medicines
That my mother showed me,
If all these fail
I go to the medicine woman,
And when the child has improved
I take a chicken to the herbalist,
Or a goat or a ram.

★

When fevers trouble my child
    frequently,
When all the diseases
Have fallen in love with him,

And all youthful diseases
Run after him
As if he was a beautiful girl,
So that he has coughs and
   dysentery
And throat trouble and eye
   sickness,
And his ears have pus
And his legs have ulcers
And he is bony, skinny
And his loin-string is loose,
I know that this is not for
   nothing!

I know that someone is behind
   it.
I know someone has hidden
The child's excreta in a tree
   fork,
Or has buried his hair or nail
   paring
In a river-bed
I know that some jealous woman
Perhaps even a close relative
Has visited the shadow trapper
Who has captured the child's
   shadow.

When your child is weak and
   listless,
When his energy fails him,
When he withdraws from the
   fight
For life, and gives up quickly,
It means his head has been
   captured,
And he is only a crawling corpse:

A diviner-priest must be called.

He will divine
And tell the killer,
The jealous one will be found
   out!

★

Ten beautiful girls
Are walking in single file,
Along the pathway,
They carry axes
They are going to the bush
To split firewood,
In the grass lurks
The black mamba,
Its throat burning with venom.

The first three girls walk past,
Then the fourth and fifth,
And all nine girls go by,
And your daughter
Who is at the tail of the line
Is struck!

She stands there,
The reptile refuses to unhook
   its fangs,
She drinks a whole cup of death,
She gives a brief shriek
And mumbles some farewell
To her loving mother!
Then she drops
Dead!

She lies there
As if feigning death;
Her ripe breasts lift up their
   hands
And wail aloud,
Saying,

> *No mouths will suck us!*
> *Our tips will not be tickled!*
> *Our milk will rot in the earth!*

In battle
The hottest youths fight at the
  front,
Eager, angry, proud,
The youths think of their loves
And say,
It is the old ones
Who die in bed!
The spears of the foe
And their arrows
Rain like the hailstones,
Your son is struck
In the small of the back,
And the spear
Cuts through the liver
And the heart.

Other people's boys receive
  bruises
Others get cuts,
Many earn battle honours,
They return home
Blowing their horns, loud and
  clear!

And while others eclebrate
And sing war songs,
You sing songs of praise,
Farewell songs to the dead!

Why should lightning
Seek out your husband
From his bedroom?
Other women's husbands
Are walking in the rain!

What is so sweet in your
  husband?
What so bitter in other people's
  sons?

Why, at the hunt,
Does the wounded buffalo bull
Charge your father
And with its blunt horn
Tear open his belly,
Throwing the intestines
On top of the grass?
Why should you
And not somebody else
Be made orphan?

★

All misfortunes have a root,
The snake bite, the spear of
  the enemy,
Lightning and the blunt buffalo
  horn,
These are the bitter fruits
Grown on the tree of Fate.
They do not fall anyhow,
They do not fall at random,
They do not come our way by
  accident,
We do not just run into them.
When your uncle curses you
You piss in your bed!
And you go on pissing in your
  bed
Until you have taken him
A white cock!

When your mother lifts her
  breast

And asks you,
Did you suck this?
If your father lifts his penis
Towards you!
Know that you are in deep
    trouble.

No one wrestles with his father,
No one looks down
On his mother,
You cannot abuse your mother!
Because it was that woman
Who hewed you out of the rock
And moulded your head and
    body.

Think of the excreta and piss
The vomit and mucus
With which you wetted your
    mother!
Think of the fire
That burnt her finger many
    times,
When she cooked for you.

Think of the jealousies of
    others,
The sorcerers and shadow
    trappers,
Poisoners and the Evil Eyes,
Think of the fights
They put up for you!

You sucked those wrinkled
    breasts,
And that's what made you
The big man you are!

And even if your father is totally
    blind,

Even if his ears are dead,
Even if the world has boxed him,
Even if his legs are dry like
    firewood,
If he is rude to you
You say, 'Thank You'
And never answer back
Because he stands before you
Like the giant *tido* tree.
You are but a climber plant.

A mother's anger is bitter,
It is fierce like lightning
And boils like thunder.
If you make her angry
She will strike below her belly
    button,
If you annoy the girl
She will strike the ash
Then you will get
Exactly what you ask for!

Your vitality will go,
You will behave
As if you were a half-wit,
Your manhood will disappear
And like a castrated bullock
Women will be perfectly safe
    with you!

And to recover,
A goat must be slaughtered,
Your mother and her brother
Must spit blessing in your hand.
And then you will become a
    man again.
There is no medicine in the
    hospital
For a mother's curse,

99

None for an uncle's curse!
And when your father's anger
Has boiled over
The white man's medicines
Are irrelevant and useless
Like the freak rains
In the middle of the dry season.

★

When a woman has brought
Death in a bundle,
With which to kill people,
And Death has felt the inside
   of the victims
And found them clean,
It bounces back
And destroys the bringer!
It refuses to be returned,
It refuses all sacrifices.
It says
'I was not brought
To eat a goat,
I do not want a ram,
Not a bull.'

Death in the bundle
Kills the children of the bringer,
Her husband,
Her other relatives
And then she herself
Eats the dust.
Which white man's medicine
Can stop the hand of Death in
   the bundle?
Which one can blunt
The sharp edges of Death's
   sword?

★

If in a hunt
The spears of the men
Strike tree trunks and earth
And they return home
Silent,
None blowing a horn,

If in the homestead
Young wives stay young,
Their breasts refuse to fall
And their tummies are for ever
Well back,
Because they are hard
Like the *lela* rocks
Like the dry trunk of the *poi*,
And the men are soft in the
   knees
And weak in the loin,

When the rains fail
And famine threatens a fierce
   invasion,
Fiercer than the spear of the
   Lango,

If the crops are moved down by
   Okwil
Or the hail stones have rained
And ruined all the millet,

If the locust swarms
That blacken the sky
Stay the night in the homestead
And refuse to move
The next day,
When there is much trouble
In the homestead,
It is not for nothing,
It is because

The ancestors are angry,
Because they are hungry,
Thirsty,
Neglected.

So the elders gather
At the clan shrine,
Blood, meat and beer
Are offered to the ancestors.
Greetings are exchanged
And the living
Pray to the dead
To cleanse the homestead,
And they pray,
Saying,

> *The troubles in the homestead*
> *Let the setting sun*
> *Go down with them!*

And the people repeat

> *Let them go down*
> *Let them go down*
> *With the setting sun!*

And an old woman
Will bless the young men,
She will spit blessing in their
   hands
So that their spears may be
   sharp,
Sharp and hard,
So that their trusted spears
Should not sleep outside
In the dewy cold,
But should strike the death spot
Deep and painful!
Then the young cobs

Will scream
And shed tears of sweet pains!

★

My husband rejects me
Because he says
That I am a mere pagan
And I believe in the devil.
He says
I do not know
The rules of health,
And I mix up
Matters of health and
   superstitions.

Ocol troubles my head,
He talks too much
And he heaps insults on me
As well as my relatives.

But most of his words are
   senseless,
They are like the songs
Of children's plays.
And he treats his clansmen
As if they are enemies.
Ocol behaves
As if he is a witch!

It is true
White man's medicines are
   strong,
But Acoli medicines
Are also strong.

The sick gets cured
Because his time has not yet
   come:

Song of Lawino

But when the day has dawned
For the journey to Pagak
No one can stop you,
White man's medicines
Acoli medicines,
Crucifixes, rosaries,
Toes of edible rats,
The horn of the rhinoceros
None of them can block the
      path
That goes to Pagak!

When Death comes
To fetch you
She comes unannounced,
She comes suddenly
Like the vomit of dogs,
And when She comes
The wind keeps blowing
The birds go on singing
And the flowers
Do not hang their heads.
The *agoga* bird is silent
The *agoga* comes afterwards,
He sings to tell
That Death has been that way!

When Mother Death comes
She whispers
Come,
And you stand up
And follow
You get up immediately,
And you start walking
Without brushing the dust
On your buttocks.

You may be behind
A new buffalo-hide shield,

And at the mock-fight
Or in battle
You may be matchless;

You may be hiding
In the hole
Of the smallest black insect,
Or in the darkest place
Where rats breast-feed their
      puppies,
or behind the Agoro hills,

You may be the fastest runner,
A long distance runner,
But when Death comes
To fetch you
You do not resist,
You must not resist.
You cannot resist!

Mother Death
She says to her little ones,
Come!

Her little ones are good children,
Obedient,
Loyal,
And when Mother Death calls
Her little ones jump,
They jump gladly
For she calls
And offers simsim paste
Mixed with honey!
She says
My only child
Come,
Come, let us go.
Let us go
And eat white-ants' paste

Mixed with *shea*-butter!
And who can resist that?

White diviner priests,
Acoli herbalists,
All medicine men and medicine
    women

Are good, are brilliant
When the day has not yet
    dawned
For the great journey
The last safari
To Pagak.

II

The Buffalos of Poverty Knock the People Down

With the coming
Of the new political parties,
My husband roams the country-
    side
Like a wild goat;

He is up before dawn:
You think
He is going to hoe
The new cotton field
Or to sow the millet
Or to harvest the simsim
All day long
He is away,
He does not eat at home
As if I do not cook!

When he comes
He does not stay a moment,
He says
There is another meeting
At the homestead of the Hoe
    Chief.

He is away all night,
And when he returns so late
He says
Their car got stuck
In the mud.

★

He says
They are fighting for Uhuru
He says
They want Independence and
    Peace
And when they meet
They shout 'Uhuru! Uhuru!'
But what is the meaning
Of Uhuru?

He says
They want to unite the Acoli
    and Lango
And the Madi and Lugbara
Should live together in peace!

He says
The Alur and Iteso and Baganda
And the Banyankole and
    Banyoro
Should be united together
With the Jo-pa-Dhola and the
    Toro
And all the tribes
Should become one people.

He says
White men must return
To their own homes,
Because they have brought
Slave conditions in the country.
He says
White people tell lies,
That they are good
At telling lies,
Like men wooing women.
Ocol says
They reject the famine relief
    granaries
And the forced-labour system.

★

I do not understand
The new political parties.
They dress differently,
They dress in robes
Like the Christian diviner-
    priests,
But Ocol treats his brother
As if they are not relatives,

Ocol puts on a green-and-white
    robe,
A large flowing robe

And he struts
Like a bull baboon,
He blows the whistle
And rings the bell
Calling people to gather
At the marketplace.

His brother wears a red-and-
    black robe,
He looks like the judge
Who condemns people to death
He looks like the male *aribe* bird
And shouts like the train.
He walks majestically
Like a bull elephant.

My husband is the leader
Of the Democratic Party.
When they greet each other
They shake their fists.

Ocol does not enter
His brother's house.
You would think
There was homicide between
    them
That has not been settled,
You would think
That the *oput*-drinking peace-
    making ceremony
Has not yet taken place
And they fear the deadly *ojebu*
    taboo!

Ocol dislikes his brother fiercely,
His mother's son's hatred
Resembles boiling oil!
The new parties have split the
    homestead
As the battle axe splits the skull!

My husband has sternly warned
  me
Never to joke
With my husband-in-law:
Not that joking may cause
  pregnancy,
Not that I am a loose woman,
But that the strong gum of the
  joke
Will reconnect the snapped
  string
Of brotherhood
Between him and his brother!

Is this the unity of Uhuru?
Is this the Peace
That Independence brings?

When my husband
Opens a quarrel
With his brother
I am frightened!
You would think
They have not slept
In the same womb,
You would think
They have not shared
The same breasts!
And they say
When the two were boys
Looking after the goats
They were as close to each other
As the eye and the nose,
They were like twins,
And they shared everything
Even a single white ant.

★

Ocol says
His brother is a liar
And a big fool.
He says
There is something wrong
With his brother's head
Nobody should trust such a beast.

He says
His brother wants to kill him,
He calls his mother's son That
  Man!
He says
His brother is dangerously
  jealous of him
And has smuggled a pistol,
And has collected money
And hired a man
To bump him off!
When Ocol says these things
His eyes bulge in his head
Like ripe papayas
And threaten to fall off!

He shouts
His brother will bring
  Communism!
I do not know
What this animal is!

He says
The Congress Party
Will remove all Catholics
From their jobs
And they will take away
All the land and schools
And will take people's wives
And goats, and chickens and
  bicycles,

105

All will become the property
Of the Congress people.

How terrible that would be
If it were true!
But I know
That if Ocol dies
His mother's son
Whom he now hates so much
Will inherit all Ocol's properties,
The goats, the chickens and the
    bicycles,
And I will become his wife
And my children will become
    his children!

Where will he take the land
And the schools?
And if they remove
All Catholics from their jobs,
Who will do the jobs?
Where will they get the people
To do these jobs?

★

When Ocol's brother replies,
He sound like the dance-drums
In the late evening.
He says
The Democratic Party
Is the Party for Padrés
The Party for fools and
    blockheads.
He says
Catholics have numb heads
They hear everything from the
    Italian Fathers!

He says
The Democratic Party
Will sell the land
To poor white men
Refugees, who came to this
    country
Saying they have come to teach
The white man's religion
When they have no teaching
    certificates.

He says
Ocol and the other fools
Allow their heads to be numbed
By foolish prayers
And by kneeling
Before white men!

I have never seen
A white padré
In the Democratic Party!
At the market place meetings
There are many Catholics
But I have not heard an Italian
Shout 'D – P! D – P! Uhuru!'
Do they teach the leaders
In the dead of night
In the Bishop's house?

And if the white men are poor
Where will they get the money
With which to buy the land?

I have seen
Many leaders of the D.P.
They come to my house
And eat and drink there,
Some have really numbed heads
Like the head of my husband;

But others have heads like
   lightning
Quick and powerful,
Some are real men
Not women dressed in dark
   suits.

I have met
Many leaders of Congress
They go to Ocol's brother's
   house
They eat and drink there.
Some have heads like the sun
Bright, burning and brilliant,
Others carry pieces of stone
On their necks
And call them heads!

★

Where is the Peace of Uhuru?
Where the unity of Indepen-
   dence?
Must it not begin at home?
And the Acoli and Lango
And the Madi and Lugbara,
How can they unite?
And all the tribes of Uganda
How can they become one?

I do not understand
The meaning of Uhuru!
I do not understand
Why all the bitterness
And the cruelty
And the cowardice,
The fear,
The deadly fear that
Eats the hearts

Of the political leaders!

Is it the money?
Is it the competition for position?

Someone said
Independence falls like a bull
   buffalo
And the hunters
Rush to it with drawn knives,
Sharp shining knives
For carving the carcass.
And if your chest
Is small, bony and weak
They push you off,
And if your knife is blunt
You get the dung on your
   elbow,
You come home empty-handed
And the dogs bark at you!

If you are not a man
They frighten you with noise
But you return home,
You walk like a chicken
Beaten by the rain
And the women hiss at you
And your children run away
   from you!
You are silent
Like a woman who has broken a
   taboo!

And the other men
Carry large pieces of fatty beef,
You hear their horns loud and
   proud!

And you eat green vegetables

Without the simsim paste
And your thin children
Collect the *odir* and *ocenne*
   insects
And they roast the *odir* and
   ocenne
And eat them
And the children of others
Are fat,
And their wives grow larger
   buttocks,
They eat meat from the chest of
   bulls
And the skin of their legs
Shines with health!

The stomach seems to be
A powerful force
For joining political parties,
Especially when the purse
In the trouser pocket
Carries only the coins
With holes in their middle,
And no purple notes
Have ever been folded in it;

And especially for those who
Have never tasted honey from
   childhood,
And those who grew up
Fatherless or motherless!
And those with no sure jobs!

Men with soft hearts,
Men with soft blunt eyes
Who are shy to tell the biggest
   lies,
Who are afraid
To repeat them in the presence

Of their mothers and children,
To repeat empty lies
Before their wives
And before their wives' mothers,
Such soft-necked men
Should stay at home!

★

And when the Party leaders
Come from Kampala,
My husband jumps,
He is like a newly eloped girl,

He is all over the place
He is quick to win a good name,
And when he talks,
He explodes like the dry pods
   of *cooro*!
He is like a woman
Who has just buried
The other woman
With whom she shares a
   husband.

He says to the bosses
'O chief you kill me with
   laughter!'
His shallow laugh and put up
   smiles
Drown the frowns of the chiefs!
They probably think he is
   wonderful!

My husband accuses other party
   leaders.
Everybody else is useless,
He alone
Is the most hard working,

The most loyal,
The man with the most reliable
    information.
All that others say
Is lies,
Lies intended only to win
    favours!
To buy position
To buy jobs
And places in conferences
In Kampala and abroad!

My husband says
The masses of the people
In the villages
Listen only to him.
He says
The other party leaders
Have formed a new party,
A new party for fools,
That they are rebels
And should be expelled!
He says
The rebels are a minority
The masses of the people
Are solidly behind him
And the Party Leaders,
And they talk about him
At all beer parties.

When my husband
Climbs onto the platform,
You hear the bell
You hear the drums!
There is a big crowd,
Some people stand on hillocks!
The crowd resembles

The Palaro gathered to
Celebrate Lapul, their chiefdom
    Jok.

My husband
Reads his speech from a book,
He says a few words
And shakes his fly whisk,
The women yodel
And make ululation!

They yodel and make ululation
Not because they understand,
They yodel so that their voices
    may be heard
So that their secret lovers may
    hear them,
They shout and make ululations
Because they are tired
Tired of the useless talk
Tired of the insults
And the lies of
The speakers.

They shout and raise their
    hands
Not because they understand
But because they do not
    understand
The many foreign words.
Uhuru! Congress! Freedom!
Democratic! Independence!
Minister! ...

The women make ululations
Because they are irritated
Because they are excited
Because they want to dance.
They want the talks to end

So that they can dance.
And when he is in the market
    place,
He talks endlessly
Like a bird's mother-in-law.
His words are itchy like scabies,
Itchy like scabies on the
    buttocks.

He talks endlessly,
And some of the things he says
Are painful and hurtful,
Like an unripe boil.

He shouts and shouts
And loses his voice.
He says
We must all unite
And fight for Independence and
    Peace.

He says
They fight with diseases,
Poverty and ignorance.
They want peace and friendship,
They fight black-heartedness
    and quarrels!

★

And if you are ignorant
Of the death of the homestead
Of my husband,
The death of the homestead
Caused by the parties
You would think
My husband was the best leader.

And while those inside

Eat thick honey
And ghee and butter,
Those in the countryside
Die with the smell,
They re-eat the bones
That were thrown away
For the dogs.

And those who have
Fallen into things
Throw themselves into soft beds,
But the hip bones of the voters
Grow painful
Sleeping on the same earth
They slept
Before Uhuru!
And they cover the ulcers
On their legs
With animal skins.

And when they have
Fallen into things
They become rare,
Like the python
With a bull water buck
In its tummy,
They hibernate and stay away
And eat!

They return
To the countryside
For the next elections
Like the kite
That returns during the Dry
    Season

*When the kites have returned
The Dry Season has come!*

★

The Democratic Party
How does it differ
From the Congress?

Ocol says
They want Uhuru,
His brother says
They want Uhuru and Peace,
Both of them say
They fight ignorance and disease!

Then why do they not join
    hands,
Why do they split up the army
Into two hostile groups?
The spears of the young men
And their shields,
Why are the weapons
And the men and women
Dispersed so uselessly?

And while the pythons of
    sickness
Swallow the children
And the buffaloes of poverty
Knock the people down
And ignorance stands there
Like an elephant,

The war leaders
Are tightly locked in bloody
    feuds,
Eating each other's liver
As if the D.P. was leprosy

And the Congress yaws;
If only the parties
Would fight poverty
With the fury
With which they fight each
    other,
If diseases and ignorance
Were assaulted
With the deadly vengeance
With which Ocol assaults his
    mother's son,
The enemies would have been
Greatly reduced by now.

★

I am concerned
About the well-being of our
    homestead!
The women there
Wear mourning clothes
The homestead is surely dead
The enmity, the black-
    heartedness,
The quarrels, the jealousies ...

When the fiends
That sow smallpox
Go through our homestead
That people will be finished,
Because the insides of the
    people are bad!
This will be the gift
That the political parties have
    brought!

And while the pythons of sickness
Swallow the children
And the buffaloes of poverty
Knock the people down

And ignorance stands there
Like an elephant,/The warleaders
Are tightly locked in bloody feuds,
Eating each other's liver ...

12

My Husband's House is a Dark Forest of Books

Listen, my clansmen,
I cry over my husband
Whose head is lost.
Ocol has lost his head
In the forest of books.

When my husband
Was still wooing me
His eyes were still alive,
His ears were still unblocked,
Ocol had not yet become a fool
My friend was a man then!

He had not yet become a
    woman,
He was still a free man,
His heart was still his chief.

My husband was still a Black
    man
The son of the Bull
The son of Agik
The woman from Okol
Was still a man,
An Acoli.

★

My husband has read much,

He has read extensively and
    deeply,
He has read among white men
And he is clever like white men

And the reading
Has killed my man,
In the ways of his people
He has become
A stump.

He abuses all things Acoli,
He says
The ways of black people
Are black
Because his eyeballs have
    exploded,
And he wears dark glasses,
My husband's house
Is a dark forest of books.
Some stand there
Tall and huge
Like the *tido* tree

Some are old
Their barks are peeling off
And they smell strongly.
Some are thin and soft.

The backs of some books
Are hard like the rocky stem of
    the *poi* tree,
Some are green
Others red as blood
Some books are black and oily,
Their backs shine like
The dangerous *ororo* snake
Coiled on a tree top.

Some have pictures on their
    backs,
Dead faces of witch-looking men
    and women,
Unshaven, bold, fat-stomached
Bony-cheeked, angry revengeful-
    looking people,
Pictures of men and women
Who died long ago.

★

The papers on my husband's
    desk
Coil threateningly
Like the giant forest climbers,
Like the *kituba* tree
That squeezes other trees to
    death;
Some stand up,
Others lie on their backs,
They are interlocked
Like the legs of youths
At the *orak* dance,
Like the legs of the planks
Of the *goggo* fence,
They are tightly interlocked
Like the legs of the giant forest
    climbers

In the impenetrable forest

My husband's house
Is a mighty forest of books,
Dark it is and very damp,
The steam rising from the ground
Hot thick and poisonous
Mingles with the corrosive dew
And the rain drops
That have collected in the
    leaves.

They choke you
If you stay there long,
They ruin your nose and tongue
So that you can no longer
Enjoy the fresh smell of simsim
    oil
Or the taste of *malakwang*;

And the boiling darkness
Bursts your eye balls.
And the sticky juices
That drop from the gum trees
Block the holes of your ears,
And when ten girls
Standing on the hillock
In the moonlight
Sing *oyele* songs,
Throwing stones of abuse
At the rough-skinned ugly old
    men
Chosen for them as husbands
By their money-loving fathers,

Or when your daughter
Sings a lovely lullaby
To her baby brother
Strapped on her back,

And she sways forwards and
    backwards
As she sings

> *O baby*
> *Why do you cry?*
> *Are you ill?*
> *O baby stop crying*
> *Your mother has fried the*
>   *aluru birds*
> *In ghee!*

When the girls sing *cycle* songs
And the nurse sings her lullaby
You hear only noises,
Noises that disturb you
Like a brick
Thrown on top of the iron roof.

★

If you stay
In my husband's house long,
The ghosts of the dead men
That people this dark forest,
The ghosts of the many white
    men
And white women
That scream whenever you
    touch any book,
The deadly vengeance ghosts
Of the writers
Will capture your head,
And like my husband
You will become
A walking corpse.

My husband's ears are numb,
He hears the crackling sounds

Of the gums within the holes of
    his ears
And thinks this is the music
Of his people;
He cannot hear
The insults of foreigners
Who say
The songs of black men are
    rubbish!

★

Listen, my husband,
Hear my cry!
You may not know this
You may not feel so,
But you behave like
A dog of the white man!
A good dog pleases its master,
It barks at night
And hunts in the salt lick
It chases away wild cats
That come to steal the chicken!
And when the master calls
It folds its tail between the legs.

The dogs of white men
Are well trained
And they understand English!

When the master is eating
They lie by the door
And keep guard
While waiting for left-overs.

But oh! Ocol
You are my master and my
    husband,
You are the father of these
    children

Song of Lawino

You are a man,
You are you!

Do you not feel ashamed
Behaving like another man's dog
Before your own wife and
    children?

My husband, Ocol
You are a Prince
Of an ancient chiefdom,
Look,
There in the middle of the
    homestead
Stands your grandfather's
    Shrine,
Your grandfather was a Bull
    among men
And although he died long ago
His name still blows like a horn,
His name is still heard
Throughout the land.

When he died
Your father proudly
Built him that Shrine!
A true son of his father
He carried out all the duties
Of a first-born son.

He himself was a great chief
Well beloved by his people.
At the *otole* dance
He was right in the middle
Completely surrounded by his
    host
Like the termite queen mother,
But you could spot him
By his huge head-gear

Waving like a field of flowering
    sugar-cane.

In battle he fought at the front
Fierce like a wounded
    buffalo-girl,
When his men struck the enemy
The heaven shook from its base;

Has the Fire produced Ash?
Has the Bull died without a
    Head?
Aaa! A certain man
Has no millet field,
He lives on borrowed foods.
He borrows the clothes he wears
And the ideas in his head
And his actions and behaviour
Are to please somebody else.
Like a woman trying to please
    her husband!
My husband has become a
    woman!

Then why do you wear a shirt?
Why do you not tie
A sheet round your waist
As other women do?
Put on the string skirt
And some beads on your loins!

★

O, my clansmen,
Let us all cry together!
Come,
Let us mourn the death of my
    husband,
The death of a Prince
The Ash that was produced

By a great Fire!
O, this homestead is utterly
   dead,
Close the gates
With *lacari* thorns,
For the Prince
The heir to the Stool is lost!
And all the young men
Have perished in the
   wilderness!
And the fame of this homestead
That once blazed like a wild fire
In a moonless night
Is now like the last breaths
Of a dying old man!

There is not one single true son
   left,
The entire village
Has fallen into the hands

Of war captives and slaves!
Perhaps one of our boys
Escaped with his life!
Perhaps he is hiding in the bush
Waiting for the sun to set!

But will he come
Before the next mourning?
Will he arrive in time?

Bile burns my inside!
I feel like vomiting!

For all our young men
Were finished in the forest,
Their manhood was finished
In the class-rooms,
Their testicles
Were smashed
With large books!

13

*Let Them Prepare
the Malakwang Dish*

But Ocol, my husband,
If you are not yet utterly dead
And fit only for the stomach
   of the earth,
If your heart-string
Is not yet completely cut,
If your ghost
Has not yet escaped and got
   completely lost,

If some blood is still flowing
However faintly,
Take courage,
Take a small amount of millet
   porridge,
Let them prop you up,
Drink some fish soup
Slowly, slowly
You will recover.

117

Chew the roots of *omwombye*.
It is very bitter
But it will clear your throat.

Let them prepare the
    malakwang dish
Eat the roots of *lurono*
And the roots of your tongue
Will be loosened.
When they have prepared *lukut*,
Eat it,
It will strengthen your knee!

Let them drop simsim oil
Into the holes of your ear,
Let them scoop out the gum
That has filled your ears for so
    long,
The thick dust you collected
From the altar
And the chaff
From the books
And the useless things
From the magazines and
    newspapers,
And the radio and television!
Here is some water.
It is luke-warm,
It will not burn you,
Let me pour it for you
So that you may wash your
    face!

But first
Remove those dark glasses,
Throw them away,
Then remove the scales
That have formed on your eyes
During daylight

When you closed your eyes
In prayer.

Bring the ripe seeds of *labikka*
And scratch Ocol's eyeballs
And remove the blood
That has clotted there,
Put the rhino-horn powder
In his eyes,
Let it stab away
The pus that blocks his eyes!

The blindness that you got in
    the library
Will be removed by the diviner!

The swelling that has blocked
    your throat
Will be treated with the shoots
    of *lapena*
Chew the shoots of *lapena* and
    olim,
Put some salt in the shoots
And swallow the bitter green
    juice!
You must vomit
The shyness you ate in the
    church.
Drink raw eggs mixed in millet
    flour; and if this does not
    make you feel sick
Put one finger
Deep down your throat!

Clean your teeth with sand,
I will prepare the sand for you
White like the sand
Vomited by the frog!

Brush your tongue
So thickly coated with bitter
    insults;
Here is warm water
There is some salt in it,
Gargle it,
Clean your mouth,
Spit out the insults with the
    water!
The abuses you learnt
From your white masters
And the stupid stubbornness
Spit them down with the water.

★

And, son of the Bull
When you are completely cured
When you have gained your full
    strength
Go to the shrine of your fathers,
Prepare a feast,
Give blood to your ancestors,
Give them beer, meat and
    millet bread,
Let the elders
Spit blessing on you
Let them intercede for you
And pray to the ancestors
Who sleep in their tombs
Face upwards.

Beg forgiveness from them
And ask them to give you
A new spear
A new spear with a sharp and
    hard point.
A spear that will crack the rock.

Ask for a spear that you will
    trust
One that does not bend easily
Like the earth-worm.
Ask them to restore your
    manhood!
For I am sick
Of sharing a bed with a woman!

Ask them to forgive
Your past stupidity,
Pray that the setting sun
May take away all your shyness
Deceit, childish pride, and
    sharp tongue!

For when you insulted me,
Saying
I was a mere village girl,
You were insulting your
    grandfathers
And grandmothers, your father
    and mother!
When you compared me
With the silly *ojuu* insects
That sit on the beer pot,
You were abusing your entire
    people.
You were saying
The customs of your people
Are like the useless things
Left in the old homestead.

When you took the axe
And threatened to cut the
    Okango
That grows on the ancestral
    shrine
You were threatening

Song of Lawino

To cut yourself loose,
To be tossed by the winds
This way and that way
Like the dead dry leaves
Of the *olam* tree
In the dry season.

When you have recovered
    properly,
Go to your old mother
And ask forgiveness from her;
Let her spit blessing in your
    hands;
And rub the saliva
On your chest
And on your forehead!

★

And I as your first wife,
Mother of your first-born,
Mother of your son and
    daughter,
I have only one request.
I do not ask for money
Although I have need of it,
I do not ask for meat,
I can live on green vegetables
For a while yet.
Buy clothes for the woman
With whom I share you,
Buy beads for her, and
    perfume;
And shoes and necklaces, and
    ear-rings!

When you have gained your full
    strength
I have only one request,
And all I ask is

That you remove the road block
From my path.

Here is my bow-harp
Let me sing greetings to you,
Let me play for you one song
    only
Let me play and sing
The song of my youth:

> She has taken the road to
>   Nimule
> She will come back tomorrow
> His eyes are fixed on the road
> Saying, Bring Alyeka to me
> That I may see her
> The daughter of the Bull
> Has stayed away too long
> His eyes are fixed on the road

All I ask
Is that you give me one chance,
Let me praise you
Son of the chief!
Tie ankle bells on my legs
Bring *lacucuku* rattles
And tie them on my legs,
Call the *nanga* players
And let them play
And let them sing,

Let me dance before you,
My love,
Let me show you
The wealth in your house,
Ocol my husband,
Son of the Bull,
Let no one uproot the
    Pumpkin.

Song of Ocol

I

Woman,
Shut up!
Pack your things
Go!

Take all the clothes
I bought you
The beads, necklaces
And the remains
Of the utensils,
I need no second-hand things.

There is a large sack
In the boot
Of the car,
Take it
Put all your things in it
And go!

Song of the woman
Is the confused noise
Made by the ram
After the butcher's knife
Has sunk past
The wind pipe,
Red paint spraying
On the grasses;
It is a song all alone
A solo fragment
With no chorus
No accompaniment,

A strange melody
Impossible to orchestrate;

As if in echo
Of women's wailing
At yesterday's funeral,
Song of the dead
Out of an old tomb,
Stealthy cracking
Of dry bones,
Falling in of skulls
Under the weight
Of earth;
It's the dull thud
Of the wooden arrow
As it strikes the concrete
Of a wall
And falls to earth,
Extinguished
Without life
Like a bird
Hit by stone
From a boy's catapult.

★

Have you heard
The sigh of a monarch
In exile?

He squats on a log

121

In the shadow
Of a disused hut,
It is cold
The keen wind
Knifes through his
Torn trousers
Licking his bruised knee
With rough fenile tongue,

Yesternight!
Yesternight ah!

The smallest toe
On the left foot
Slowly weeps blood,
A fat house-fly
Drones away;

Under the arm-pit
It is sticky,
The remains of a shirt
Sticks to his back,

Yesternight ah!
The hot bath
The thick purple carpet,
The red slippers ...

His dry lips taste salty,
A ball of thirst
Is climbing up his throat
He is forcing down
Some saliva,

Yesternight
The waiter on his knees,
The woman whispering,
'My Lord, My husband',
The red wine

The soft lights,
Woman's smile
Inviting man to bed,
The hot lips
Of her younger sister
Firm breasts
The embrace ...

He looks at his hands
At the black finger nails,
Cold sweat ...
He is choking,
He keeps asking himself,
'But why? Why? Why?'

★

Song of the woman
Is the mad bragging
Of a defeated General,
Ten thousand men
Dead, dying,
The others scattered;

It is the pointless defiance
Of the condemned,
He is blindfolded,
The rough hand
Of the noose
Round his neck.

★

Woman
Your song
Is rotting buffalo
Left behind by
Fleeing poachers,
Its nose blocked

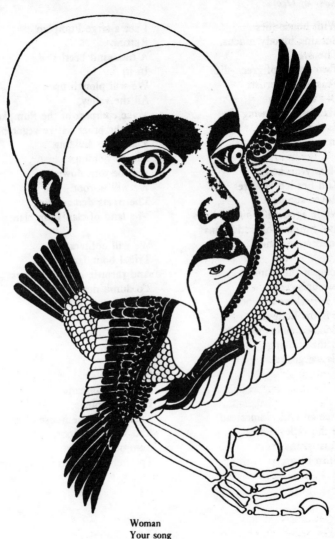

Woman
Your song
Is rotting buffalo
Left behind by
Fleeing poachers

Song of Ocol

With house-flies
Sucking bloody mucus,
The eyes
Two lumps of green-flies
Feasting on crusts
Of salty tears,
Maggots wallowing
In the pus
In the spear wounds;

Skinny-necked
Bald headed vultures
Hover above,
While aged stiff-jointed lions
And limping-hipped hyenas
Snarl over bones;

Song of the woman
Is sour sweet,
It is pork gone rancid,
It is the honeyed
Bloodied sour milk
In the stinking
Maasai gourd.

★

I see an Old Homestead
In the valley below
Huts, granaries ...
All in ruins;

I see a large Pumpkin
Rotting
A thousand beetles
In it;
We will plough up
All the valley,
Make compost of the Pumpkins
And the other native vegetables,
The fence dividing
Family holdings
Will be torn down,
We will uproot
The treets demarcating
The land of clan from clan,

We will obliterate
Tribal boundaries
And throttle native tongues
To dumb death.

★

Houseboy,
Listen
Call the *ayah*
Help the woman
Pack her things,
Then sweep the house clean
And wash the floor,
I am off to Town
To fetch the painter.

2

What is Africa
To me?

Blackness,
Deep, deep fathomless
Darkness;

Africa,
Idle giant
Basking in the sun,
Sleeping, snoring,
Twitching in dreams;

Diseased with a chronic illness,
Choking with black ignorance,
Chained to the rock
Of poverty,

And yet laughing,
Always laughing and dancing,
The chains on his legs
Jangling;

Displaying his white teeth
In bright pink gum,
Loose white teeth
That cannot bite,
Joking, giggling, dancing ...

Stuck in the stagnant mud
Of superstitions,
Frightened by the spirits
Of the bush, the stream,

The rock,
Scared of corpses ...

He hears eerie noises
From the lakeside
And from the mountain top,
Sees snakes
In the whirlwind
And at both ends
Of the rainbow;

The caves house his gods
Or he carries them
On his head
Or on his shoulder
As he roams the wilderness,
Led by his cattle,
Or following the spoor
Of the elephant
That he has speared
But could not kill;

Child,
Lover of toys,
Look at his toy weapons,
His utensils, his hut ...
Toy garden, toy chickens,
Toy cattle,
Toy children ...

Timid,
Unadventurous,
Scared of the unbeaten track,

Unweaned,
Clinging to mother's milkless
    breasts
Clinging to brother,
To uncle, to clan,
To tribe

To blackness,

To Africa,

Africa
This rich granary
Of taboos, customs,
Traditions ...

Mother, mother,
Why,
Why was I born
Black?

3

To hell
With your Pumpkins
And your Old Homesteads,
To hell
With the husks
Of old traditions
And meaningless customs,

We will smash
The taboos
One by one,
Explode the basis
Of every superstition,
We will uproot
Every sacred tree
And demolish every ancestral
    shrine.

★

We will not just
Breach the wall

Of your mud hut
To let in the air,
Do you think
We plan merely
To bring light
Into the hut?
We will set it ablaze
Let fire consume it all
This liar of backwardness;

We will uproot granaries
Break up the cooking pots
And water pots,
We'll grind
The grinding stones
To powder;

That obsolete toy
With which you scratch the soil
And the other rusty toys
In the hut,

The dried fish
Riddled with cockroaches,
The piece of carcass
Hung above the cooking place
Black with soot ...
We'll make a big heap
Of all the rubbish
From the hut
And set the heap
    Aflame.

★

Look at that woman
Shaking the rattle gourd
And talking to herself,

Mad creature,
Her hair
A burnt out forest,
Her eyes
A pair of rockets
Shooting out from the head,
Serpent tongue
Spitting poisons
Lashing crocodile tail;

Do you see
The fools
Sitting around her?
Terror infested faces
Eyes closed
Gummed with tears,
Lips cracked, bleeding,
Throats
Parched deserts of drought;

That child lying
On the earth

Numb
Bombs exploding in his head,
Blood boiling
Heavy with malarial parasites
Raging through his veins,

The mad woman
Spits on the palms
Of his hands
And on his feet,
Squirts beer
On his face
To cool him,
Spills chicken blood
On his chest,
A gift to Death!

The child's mother
Smiles,
The diviner pleads
With dread malaria,

    I give you blood,
        Let this child live;
    Here's your beer
    Take your beer,
        Leave us this child;
    Take your food....

We will round up
All these priests
And priestesses of darkness,
All the rain-makers
And herbalists,
The men and women
Who sacrifice at chiefdom
Or clan shrines,

We will arrest all the witches,

Serpent tongue
Spitting poisons
Lashing crocodile tails

Wizards, evil-eyes,
Sellers of fetish bundles,
Bones and claws,
Dealers in poisons
Extracted from plants
And venoms from snakes;

We will put all these
Pillars of fear
In a lake steamer,
Take them to the deepest part
And cast them into the void;

★

We will arrest
All the village poets
Musicians and tribal dancers,
Put in detention
Folk-story tellers
And myth makers,
The sustainers of
Village morality;

We'll disband
The nest of court historians
Glorifiers of the past,
We will ban
The stupid village anthem of
  'Backwards ever
    Forwards never.'

★

To the gallows
With all the Professors
Of Anthropology

And teachers of African
  History,
A bonfire
We'll make of their works,
We'll destroy all the anthologies
Of African literature
And close down
All the schools
Of African Studies.

★

Where is Aimé Césaire?
Where Leopold Senghor?
Arrest Janheinz Jahn
And Father Placide Temples,
Put in detention
All the preachers
Of Negritude;

The balloon of
The African Personality
Exploded long ago,
DuBois is dead
We will erect
No memorial for him;
Why should I care
Who built the citadel
Of Zimbabwe?
Of what relevance is it
Whether black men
Architected the Pyramid?

Smash all these mirrors
That I may not see
The blackness of the past
From which I came
Reflected in them.

4

Noises come
From within a dark hut,
A foul smell seeps
Of crude *waragi*
And stale *kwete* beer,
Chickens are fighting
Over fresh dung of child;

It is Adok Too
The blind poet from Lamogi
Playing the *nanga*
And singing praises
To a newly wed bride;
Footsteps of men and women
Are stamping the earth,
Puffs of dust
Mingled with smoke,
Smell of burnt meat;

A woman makes ululations
A man blows
A long wooden horn,
It sounds like a sneezing hippo,
Adok Too sings softly ...

★

Ten stacks of newly split
     firewood,
Leaning against the old tree
In the middle of
The Homestead,
Five stacks of grass

For starting fire,
Five stacks of grass
For thatching a new hut,
The hut of the newly-wed:

Do you know the slave
Who split the firewood?
Show me the tractor
They used for cutting the grass
And the cart
That brought the firewood
And the grass home;

★

I see a young woman
Returning home from the well,
Balancing a large pot
On her head,
Some water spilling
Her face slimes wet
Beads of water
On her bare breasts,
Long yellow and red
Beams from the setting sun
Darting over her youthful
     breasts
Like dragon flies;

Her naked feet
Digging the pathway,
Nibbling away the earth,
Her soles are thick

Song of Ocol

Cracked like the earth
In the dry season,
The skin of her hands
Are rough like concrete wall,
There are stones
Embedded in the skin,
Her palms are worn out
Like the soles
Of old shoes;

★

The blind poet's voice
Is piercing the thatch,
The arrow of his song
Strikes the woman
Like lightning:

O! daughter of Bull
Wild lily of the hills
You are fit for son of Chief,
O! my brother
A dream deceived me,
What an envious dream?
When I woke
I was wet ...

★

Sister
Woman of Acoliland
Throw down that pot
With its water,
Let it break into pieces
Let the water cool
The thirsty earth;

It is taboo
To throw down water pots

With water in them,
But taboos must be broken,
Taboos are chains
Around the neck,
Chains of slavery;

Shatter that pot,
Shatter taboos, customs,
Traditions ...

Listen not
To the song of the poet
The blind musician
Plays for his bread,
The bread owners
Are your slavers;
Listen not to Adok Too's
    praises,
They are spurs
For the tired horses,
Blinkers for donkeys;

★

You woman from Kikuyuland
Let that burden slide,
Fall from your back
You are no mere
Donkey cart;
Cut that *mukwa* cord
Cutting a valley in your head,
Burn the *kyondo* sacks
That bow you down
To see only my dusty boots,

Lift up your head
Walk erect
My love,

131

The blind poet's voice
Is piercing the thatch,
The arrow of his song
Strikes the woman
Like lightning

Let me see
Your beautiful eyes,
Let me caress
Your sultry neck,
Let me kiss your dimples ...

Shut up you
Bush poet from Kiambu
And you from Nyeri,
Cease insulting my wife
With your stupid song
My girl is not
A camel;

Listen
My sister from Ankole
And you from Ruanda
And Burundi,

Here's a hammer,
Smash those pots
Of rotten milk
Burst open the door
Come forth into daylight,

Beat up that old woman
Who pumps you full of milk,

Are you a caterpillar
For wasps
To lay their eggs in?
Who told you
That your fertility
Will be enhanced
By excessive fatness?

Who says you are beautiful
When you cannot even walk?

You stagger into the sunlight
Melting, dripping, wet,
A pregnant hippo;
Soft, flabby, weak,
Bursting buttocks,
Your breasts are two drums,
Can you see your belly button?
I hear the lowing of cattle
A forest of long white horns
Approaching home.

I hear the wild song
Of the herdsman
He is singing praises
To your ugliness!

Woman of Africa
Sweeper
Smearing floors and walls
With cow dung and black soil,
Cook, *ayah*, the baby tied on
    your back,
Vomiting,
Washer of dishes,
Planting, weeding, harvesting,
Store-keeper, builder,
Runner of errands,
Cart, lorry,
Donkey....

Woman of Africa
What are you not?

In *buibui*
Your face is covered
In black cloth
Like a bat's leather wing,

Harem
Private collection
Of tasty flesh,
Do you hear the bell
Of the leading cow?
The dust you see
Is not caused by a hurricane,
It's the herds
Of the Jo-Lango;

We will destroy
All these *shenzi* cattle
The root of their savagery,
The cause of their misery
And death;

★

I see you husband
He's had a little drink
His mouth drooling:

    Asha before lunch
    Chausiku after dinner
    Young Akelo after
       midnight ...

★

In Buganda

They buy you
With two pots
Of beer,
The Luo trade you
For seven cows,

And what is that Madi hoe
The Acoli men give your
    father?
He cannot even use it
For digging!
They purchase you
On hire purchase even,
Like bicycles,

You are furniture,
Mattress for man
Your arm
A pillow
For his head!

★

Woman of Africa
Whatever you call yourself,
Whatever the bush poets
Call you
You are not
A wife!

5

You Karamojong elder
Etched with the scars
Of spear,
You young raiders
Skimming across the plains
Ostrich feathers dancing on
    your heads
Blown back like papyrus tufts
By the Nile,
I see blood
On the shafts
Of your spears;

You Maasai warrior
Honing your spear
And polishing it with ghee,
You naked Jie
Studying the sick cow,
You Turkana scout
Perched on the termite mound
Ijakait from Toposa,
You Dodos General
Presiding over the wár council;

You Suk youth
I hear you singing
Praises to your black ox,
Your hands raised
In imitation of its horns;

You men on Nandi hills
Tending cattle in the rocky
    pastures

Always suspecting an impending
    raid,
You Pokot hordes
Driving home the stolen cattle;

Kipsigis men
I see colourful shields
Surrounding a thick bush
In which I see
A lion's tufted tail ...

You proud Kalenjin
Chiefless, free,
Each man the chief
Of his hut.

★

When your spears
Appeared on the horizon
Beyond the Bahr el Ghazal
The Nilotes scattered
Like flying debris
From a bombed house,
The Luo ran
A thousand miles
Were stopped by the big Lake,
Had you given chase
They might have perished
In the water
Like the Egyptians
In the Red Sea;

135

When you swept Southwards
Towards the Rift Valley
Other men fled
Like antelopes
Chased by the leopard,

Like grass-hoppers
Escaping from a wild fire;

You taught Kikuyus
Circumcision,
Spread the chiefless democracy
Of the Age-Sets system ...

Kalenjin,
You Jo-Lango —
Spirit haunted,
Survey your booty,
Study your empire,
Your gains:

★

A large arc
Of semi desert land
Strewn with human skeletons
Barely covered by the
Hostile thorn bushes
And the flowering cactus,
A monument to five hundred
    years
Of cattle theft!
Wallowing in the mud
Of poverty and ignorance
You recited poems
About the beauty of your
    beasts,
Sang songs about the might
Of your spears

And your thieving exploits;

Believing you were
The richest of the earth,
Drunk with the illusion
Of real power
You continued to jump
Up and down
Up and down
As you dance,
Firmly holding to the spear,
The symbol of your
    backwardness;

You barren empire
Remained 'closed' to progress,
A vast natural animal reserve
In which wild men
And wild beasts roamed,
Students of primitive man
Big game hunters
And tourists flocked in
From all corners of the world,
White woman came to discover,
To see with their naked eyes
What manhood could be!

★

You mountain dwelling Sebei
Do you hear me?
You Kumam
Digging lung-fish
From the marshes,
You Iteso
Fighting at the beer party,
You Lutuko ...

Listen,

We will not simply
Put the Maasai in trousers
To end twenty five thousand
    years
Of human nakedness,
Dynamiting the ochre quarries
Is only the starting gun,

We will arrest
All the elders
The tutors of the young
During circumcisions,
The gathering of youths
In the wilderness for initiations
Will be banned,
The council of elders
Will be abolished;
The war dance ...
The blowing of war horns
Will be punished
With twelve strokes
Of the cane
For each blast;

All the men with *moi* names
And those with 'killer' marks
On their backs
And on their arms
Will be hanged for murder;

★

You will be disarmed,
If need be, by force,
All your spears
And colourful shields,
All your bows
And poisoned arrows
Will be destroyed,

Not one will be left
Even for the museums,

Spearmakers and blacksmiths
Will be jailed;
Ah!
What a colourful heap
We'll make
Of the ostrich feathers
And all the other head gears,
We'll reduce the heap to ashes;

We will rip off
The smelly goatskin skirts
From the women
And burn them,
Cut all the giraffe hair necklaces
And elephant hair bangles,
Break the ivory amulets
Cutting deep in the flesh
Of the upper arms,
Remove all the chains,
Ear rings, nose rings,
Lip-stops ...

Each head will be shaved ...

★

Spearing black billy goats
In the dry river bed,
Sacrifices to cool
The blood of the murdered
    man,
All superstitious activities
Will be stamped out,
They will not be allowed
Even on the stage;

★

137

Tell me
You young man
From Maasailand,
They call you *moran*,
I see your brother's spear
Planted at the door
Of your hut,
You know he is inside
Sleeping with your wife!

Would you let a man
'Borrow' your wife
Yet kill him
For taking your *shuka*?

We shall burn down
The *manyattas*,
Destroy each one of them
Together with all stupid
    customs
That are observed in them.

★

Ijakait,
Come brother,
You are tall and athletic
You are handsome,
Walk into your City

With your head up;

Do you see
The eyes of the girls
Glued on you?
Here you do not have
To kill a man or a lion first.

Take that girl
She wants you.

★

You sister
From Pokot
Who grew in the open air,
You are fresh ...
Ah!
Come,
Walk with me
In the City gardens,
Hold my hand ...
My woman
Here's a rose bud,
Keep it,
Guard it,
Don't lose it,
Do you hear?

6

Do I hear you whisper
    Who is that man?
    What is his name?
Do you not know me
And my brothers-in-power?

All the time
I was reading Econ.
At Makerere,
And my friend the Resident
    Magistrate

Was sweating and cramming for
    the Bar,
You were busy
Performing the get-stuck dance,
Spending weeks at funeral
    parties,
Or in the bush
Chasing wild animals
Or collecting wild honey,
Thoughtless and carefree
Like children dancing around
    the hut
After a meal;
We spent years
In detention
Suffering without bitterness
And planning for the
    revolution;

Tell me
My friend and comrade,
Answer me simply and frankly,

Apart from the two shillings fee
For Party membership,
And the dances you performed
When the Party chiefs
Visited your village,
And the slogans you shouted
That you did not understand,

What was your contribution
In the struggle for uhuru?

★

Comrade,
Do you not agree

That without your present
    leaders
Uhuru could never have come?

And, surely,
You are not so mean
As to grudge them
Some token reward,
Are you?

★

I have a nice house
In the Town,
My spacious garden
Explodes with jacaranda and
    roses,
I have lilies, bougainvillea,
    canna ...

Do you appreciate the beauty
Of my roses?
Or would you rather turn
My flower garden
Into a maize shamba?

★

What did you reap
When uhuru ripened
And was harvested?

Is it my fault
That you sleep
In a hut
With a leaking thatch?

Do you blame me
Because your sickly children

139

Do you appreciate the beauty
Of my roses?
Or would you rather turn
My flower garden
Into a maize shamba?

Sleep on the earth
Sharing the filthy floor
With sheep and goats?
Who says
I am responsible
For the poverty of the
    peasantry?
Am I the cause of
    unemployment
And landlessness?

Did you ever see me
Touring the countryside
Recruiting people's daughters
Into prostitution?

How did I make men ignorant?
Was it not I
Who asked the Minister
To build a school
In your village?
And did I prevent
Children from other villages
From going to school?

★

I have other properties
In the Town,
But,
Come,
Beat the dust off your feet
And jump into my Merc.,
Let me take you for a ride
And show you around my
    farm ...

When the tractor first snorted
On these hunting grounds

The natives scuttled into the
    earth
Like squirrels,
Like the edible rat
Pursued by the hunter's dog,

Behold,
Africa's wildest bush
Is now a garden green
With wheat, barley, coffee ...

Look at that prize bull,
Black, hornless and without a
    hump ...

Don't touch the udder of my
    cow
With your unsterilized hands,
Don't touch the milking
    utensils ...

Do you see
That golden carpet
Covering the hillside?
Those are my sheep ...
Wool, mutton;

O!
How refreshing it is
To watch the plants germinate,
Grow, flower and ripen,
And the young healthy animals
Playing!

I come to my farm
Every week-end,
It's wonderful to get out
Of the Town
Into the fresh air

Of the country,
I enjoy the smell
Of the earth,
The aroma of the coffee
   blossoms
Intoxicates me!

★

Tell me
My friend and comrade,
Do you remember
The night of uhuru
When the celebration drums
   throbbed
And men and women wept with
   joy
As they danced,
Hands raised in salute
To the national flag?

Did someone tell you
That on the morning of uhuru
The dew on the grass
Along the village pathways
Would turn into gold,

To be collected by the women
Going to the well
To fetch water,
Or by the early morning
   hunters
Laying traps for the duikers
At the water holes?

And the leaves
Of the *olam* tree
That fall off
At the start of the droughts,
Did you dream
That the leaves
Would become banknotes
And be scattered by the wind
Among the villagers?

★

We have property

And wealth,
We are in power;

Trespassers must be jailed
For life,
Thieves and robbers
Must be hanged,
Disloyal elements
Must be detained without
   trial . . .

★

Have lions
Begun to eat grass,
To lie down with lambs
And to play games with
   antelopes?
Can a leopardess
Suckle a piglet?

7

What do you mutter there
Idiot?
I hear you whimper
Like a sick puppy,
Your penis shrivelled up
With fear;

Listen to the beggar's song,
The song of a cripple
At sunset:

★

We sowed,
We watered
Acres of Cynicism,
Planted forests of Laughter
Bitter Laughter
Corrosive venom,
Men shed tears
As they rocked
Held their sides
Laughed, laughed,
Floods of tears
Turned red;

We manured the Land
Frustrations sprouted
Bursting the soil
Like young banana trees,
Fat Frustrations

Flourished fast

Yielding fruits
Green as gall;

On the hillsides
We planted Fear,
It's blood-red blossoms
Covered the hills
Like February fires,
Prickly leaves
Hard and yellow
Pricked men's skins
Causing festering wounds;

In the valley
A streamlet trickled,
Its water sluggish, slimy,
Beside the streamlet
The lamb
Uhuru
Dead as stone,
The shimmering flies
Giving false life
To its open eyes!

A herdsboy
Sat on the bank above,
Threw small stones
Hit the carcass,
The flies rose
Like white ants,
The boy sobbed
Eyes smarting with pepper;

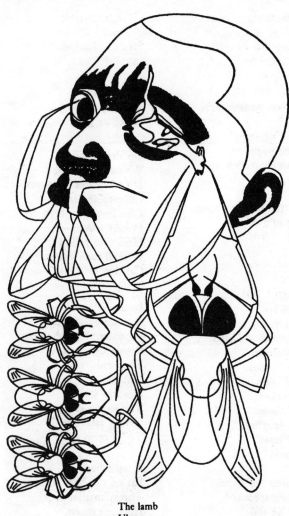

The lamb
Uhuru
Dead as Stone,
The shimmering flies
Giving false life
To its open eyes?

Two men stood
On the other side
Roared like thunder,
Peals of Laughter
Dipped in poison
Pierced the boy
Like daggers of steel,
Blood gushed from his heart
Anointing the Land!
We reaped Cynicism

Stored it
In a concrete granary
Wider, deeper
Than Mwitanzige*,
We distilled Anger
From the Laughter
Ten thousand tons
Of venom;
Stored it in a tank
Underground,
Acrid steam rose
Like lazy smoke,
Trees and grasses died;
A smouldering mound we made
Of Frustrations and Fear
Higher than Kirinyaga†
Its fiery lips
Licked the clouds,
Heaven wept;

A hunter
Sat in the shadow
Of a rock,
Rubbed two sticks
A flash,

Thunder roared,
Flames
Purified the Land!

★

Out of my way
You cowardly fool
Creep back and hide
In your mother's womb;
Vex me no more
With your hollow wailings
And crocodile tears
Over uhuru!

You Pigmy men
Skinning the elephant
With rusty knives,
I see your children
Happy, dancing,
Swinging from branch to
     branch
Like naked hairless
Black apes,

You dwarf
Rubbing two sticks
To make fire,
Which is the plant
From which you extract
Poison for the arrows?

You *mukopi*
Carrying water
For your landlord's wife,
You squatter ...

* 'Killer of locusts', Lake Albert in Uganda
† Mount Kenya

What is uhuru to you?

You Indian dukawallah
Coughing spittle onto the floor,
Your citizenship card
Nailed on the wall,
You prostitute
Sowing syphilis in the
   nightclubs
You unemployed ...

You loyal Muganda
Dressed in white *kanzu*,
I see you kneeling
Before another man,
Trailing your *kanzu*
In the mud,
Like a priest
But serving an altar of man
Not God;

You man from Bunyoro
And you from Toro
What's wrong with your knees
That you lie on your bellies
Eating dust?
Are you earthworms?

When the naked Luo,
Through trickery,
Established their rule
Over you,
And stole your cattle,
Your women, your land

And made you serfs,
For five hundred years
You continued to show
Your 'loyalties'
By performing acts of servitude;
What is uhuru to you?
You Bairu from Ankole
You slaves in Ruanda and
   Burundi,
Do I see you
Holding a beer pot
While your lofty master
Sucks the beer
Through the sucking tube?

Let that pot fall
Beer and all
Shatter and splash
Over the chief's head;

★

We will uproot
Each tree
From the Ituri forest
And blow up
Mount Kilimanjaro,
The rubble from Ruwenzori
Will fill the Valleys
Of the Rift,
We will divert
The mighty waters
Of the Nile
Into the Indian Ocean.

8

Woman
I see cups of tears
Streaming down your cheeks,
Your body shaking
With anger and despair
Like a mother
Sitting by her dead son;

Let them raise the alarm,
Sound the war drums
And blow the war horns,
Let the women make ululations,
Call all the tribesmen
And all the tribeswomen,
Let them gather together
For the last time;
Let them put ash
On their heads
And on their bodies
Let the women cry aloud
And beat their chests with
    stones,
Let them throw themselves
On the ground
And roll in the dust
And tear their hair
In mourning!
Let the men
Polish their weapons
And arm themselves with
    spears,
Shields, bows, arrows
And battle axes,

Let them wear ostrich feathers
On their heads
And swishes
On their arms,

Let them blow their horns
And their wooden trumpets,
Let the youths
Perform the mock fight
And the women shout
The praise names of their men
And of their clans
And of the clans of their
    husbands;

Let the drummers
Play the rhythms
Of the funeral dance,
And let the people sing and
    dance
And celebrate the passing of
The Old Homestead!

★

Weep long,
For the village world
That you know
And love so well,
Is gone,
Swept away
By the fierce fires
Of progress and civilization!

That walk to the well
Before sunrise,
The cool bath in the stream,
The gathering of the family
Around the evening fire ...

That shady evergreen *byeyo* tree
Under which I first met you
And told you
I wanted you,
Do you remember
The song of the *ogilo* bird
And the chorus
Of the grey monkeys
In the trees nearby?

★

Let the people drink
Kwete beer and *waragi*,
Let them suck *lacoi* beer
With the sucking tubes
As they mourn
The death of
The Old Homestead!

You village chief
Sitting on the stool
And leaning on the central pole
Of your hut,
Mount the rostrum
At the drum post,
Let the people draw near
And keep silence,

Deliver your farewell speech;
Farewell to your friends
And your age-mates,
To your sons and daughters

And to your grandchildren,
Let them bid farewell to you
And to each other,
For tomorrow morning
As the cock crows
For the first time,
The people will disperse,
Each following his or her own
    route:
Pilgrims to the New City,
And once they depart
They will never meet again!

Say Goodbye
For you will never
Hunt together again,
Nor dance the war dance
Or the *bwola* dance....

Bid farewell
To your ancestral spirits
Fleeing from the demolished
    Homestead,
With their backs to you
They can no longer hear
Your prayers,
Waste no more chicken or goat
    or sheep
As sacrifices to them,
They are gone with the wind,
Blown away with the smoke
Of the burnt Homestead!
Stop crying
You woman,
Do you think those tears
Can quench the flames
Of civilization?

Wash your face with cold water,

148

Here's soap and towel ...
Take some aspirin
It'll clear your headache ...

★

I see the great gate
Of the City flung open,
I see men and women
Walking in ...

And what are you doing there
Under the tree

Why don't you walk in
With the others?
Are you feeling homesick
For the deserted Homestead?
Or are you frightened
Of the new City?

You have only two alternatives
My sister,
Either you come in
Through the City Gate,
Or take the rope
And hang yourself!

9

Your Excellency
Bwana President
I salute you,
And you Honourable Ministers
Discussing the White Paper;
Mister Speaker, Sir,
You Backbenchers
And Opposition chiefs,
Greetings to you!

I rise
For your Lordship,
Robed, bespectacled,
I see the learned attorney
Addressing the jury,
And his brother advocate
Consulting a volume
Of the *Law Reports*
A House of Lord's judgement;

Amen!
The black Bishop
At the altar
Is blessing the people
In Latin,
Do you see his golden crown
And scarlet robe?

★

Tell me
You worshipful Mayors,
Aldermen, Councillors,
You Town Clerks in wigs,
You trade union leader
Organising the strike,
You fat black capitalist
In the dark suit,
You sipping the Scotch,

Bank manager computerising
    overdrafts,
You surgeons and physicians
At Mulago and Kenyatta
    Hospitals,
Surveyors, architects, engineers,
Accountants, broadcasters ...
You artists, novelists,
Dramatists, poets,

Military men
And you Police chiefs,
I see you
Studying the situation
And plotting the next move;

You Permanent Secretary
Composing the Minister's
    speech,
You Party leader
Standing on top of the
    Land-Rover
Addressing the market crowd,

You African Ambassador
At the United Nations,
Your Excellency
Speak,

Tell the world
In English or in French,
Talk about
The African foundation
On which we are
Building the new nations
Of Africa.

You scholar seeking after truth
I see the top

Of your bald head
Between mountains of books
Gleaming with sweat,
Can you explain
The African philosophy
On which we are reconstructing
Our new societies?

★

I hear a faint flute
Playing in the moonlight,
It is Leopold Senghor's tune
Of African Socialism,
Do you hear
That distant drum?
Is that not Mwalimu
Nyerere's *Ujamaa*?

The Osagyefo
Is silent,
The anthem of
United Africa
Is drowned by
The sound of guns!
Tell me
You student of communism,
And you Professor of History
Did Senegalese blood
Flow in the veins
Of Karl Marx?
And Lenin,
Was he born
At Arusha?

★

We shall build
A new City on the hill

Overlooking the Lake,
Concrete, steel, stone ...
The termite queen-mother
Will starve to death ...
Broad avenues, spacious
    gardens,
Parks, swimming pools ...
We will erect monuments
To the founders
Of modern Africa:
Leopold 11 of Belgium,
Bismarck ...

Streets will be named
After the great discoverers,
David Livingstone,
Henry Stanley, Speke ...
We will not forget
Karl Peters ...

'Hannington Park'
To commemorate the Bishop
Murdered by Mwanga's men,
If we can trace them
We'll hang them
For the crime.

★

You young soldier
Guarding the border post,
Do you know
When that sacred boundary
Was drawn?
Which of your ancestors
Established the area
Of your beloved

Country?
No street
Will be named
After Mansa Sulayman
Of ancient Mali,

He is as irrelevant
As the Greek goddess Artemmis,
A miserly king
He passed nothing on
To us;

Mohammed Askia
Great monarch of Songai,
What a hollow sounding name?
The Nilotic chiefs
Labongo and Gipir
Were famous for their quarrels
Over a spear
And for splitting open
A baby's belly
To retrieve a bead!

Let the kings of Ghana
Rot in the earth,
We'll forget
The rulers of Monomatapa ...

As for Shaka
The Zulu General,
How can we praise him
When he was utterly defeated
And killed by his own brothers?

What proud poem
Can we write
For the vanquished?